PRAISE FOR *INVITATION TO LEAD*

"Paul Tokunaga has hit a grand slam. All throughout this book I found myself repeatedly saying, 'That's me . . . That's exactly how I feel . . . That's exactly how I am.' Paul has captured the pulse of the Asian American leader: competent, highly skilled and gifted, with tremendous potential and possibility yet in need of encouragement, mentoring and hope. Paul provides for us the possibility of being ourselves and being effective leaders."

SOONG-CHAN RAH, SENIOR PASTOR, CAMBRIDGE COMMUNITY FELLOWSHIP CHURCH

"With insights from the Bible, Asian American experiences and his own personal journey, Paul Tokunaga has produced a work that will serve as an invaluable resource for Asian American leaders as well as for those who serve alongside them. The Asian American and the wider Christian communities have needed a book like this for a long time."

PETER CHA, ASSISTANT PROFESSOR IN PRACTICAL THEOLOGY,
TRINITY EVANGELICAL DIVINITY SCHOOL

"Weaving personal reflections with practical guidance, Paul Tokunaga provides up and coming Asian American leaders with invaluable insights on how to reach their full potential. This book offers candor and wisdom from an experienced ministry leader who shares both the ups and the downs of his own leadership journey. Read this book and accept his invitation!"

HELEN LEE, COFOUNDER, BEST CHRISTIAN WORKPLACES INSTITUTE, FORMER PUBLISHER,
RE:GENERATION QUARTERLY

"In writing this book, Paul Tokunaga has provided a compelling and comprehensive training resource for Asian American Christian leaders. Using his Japanese/Southern wit, his keen eye for observing Asian American cultural tendencies, and his own journey as an outstanding leader in many different and challenging settings, he has found ways to coax more of us also to step forward and contribute in ways that affirm who we are and will bless countless others."

REV. DR. KEN UYEDA FONG, SENIOR PASTOR, EVERGREEN BAPTIST CHURCH OF LOS ANGELES

"This book provides wonderfu⌐   ⌐bout the intersection between Asian American leaders⌐   ⌐he context of Christianity and mainstream s⌐

J. D. HOKOYAMA, PRESIDENT & ⌐
FOR ASIAN PACIFICS, INC. (LEA⌐

D1404221

invitation to Lead

Guidance

for Emerging

Asian American

Leaders

PAUL TOKUNAGA

InterVarsity Press
Downers Grove, Illinois

InterVarsity Press
P.O. Box 1400, Downers Grove, IL 60515-1426
World Wide Web: www.ivpress.com
E-mail: mail@ivpress.com

InterVarsity Press® is the book-publishing division of InterVarsity Christian Fellowship/USA®, a student movement active on campus at hundreds of universities, colleges and schools of nursing in the United States of America, and a member movement of the International Fellowship of Evangelical Students. For information about local and regional activities, write Public Relations Dept., InterVarsity Christian Fellowship/USA, 6400 Schroeder Rd., P.O. Box 7895, Madison, WI 53707-7895, or visit the IVCF website at <www.ivcf.org>.

Cover design: Maggie Wong
Cover image: Abrams/Lacagnina/Getty Images

ISBN 0-8308-2393-X

Printed in the United States of America ∞

Library of Congress Cataloging-in-Publication Data

Tokunaga, Paul.
   Invitation to lead: guidance for emerging Asian American leaders/
Paul Tokunaga.
      p. cm.
Includes bibliographical references.
   ISBN 0-8308-2393-X (pbk.: alk. paper)
   1. Leadership. 2. Leadership—Religious aspects—Christianity. 3.
Asian Americans—Psychology. I. Title.
   BF637.L4 T85 2003
   253—dc21
                                                                    2002152085

| P | 18 | 17 | 16 | 15 | 14 | 13 | 12 | 11 | 10 | 9 | 8 | 7 | 6 | 5 | 4 | 3 | 2 |
| Y | 17 | 16 | 15 | 14 | 13 | 12 | 11 | 10 | 09 | 08 | 07 | 06 | 05 | 04 | 03 |

FOR MY WIFE, MARGARET,

WHOSE PARTNERSHIP THESE PAST TWENTY-FIVE YEARS

HAS GIVEN ME THE COURAGE TO LEAD

CONTENTS

ACKNOWLEDGMENTS

To say Asian Americans are communal by nature doesn't come close to describing my experience in writing this book. Long before I started writing, fellow Asian American leaders believed and invested in me. They gave me confidence to lead in Asian American settings. Thank you Stan Inouye, Ken Fong, Donna Dong, Peter Cha, Greg Jao and Sam Barkat for being my mentors.

I have been part of InterVarsity Christian Fellowship's Asian American staff coordinating team for the past eight years. The partnership shared with members past and present gave me much to drawn upon as I wrote. Thank you Jeanette Yep, Susan Cho Van Riesen, Brad Wong, Sandy Schaupp, Collin Tomikawa, Henry Lee, James Choung and Jennifer Ikoma. Y'all rock. I'm also grateful to J. D. Hokoyama and the staff of Leadership Education for Asian Pacifics (LEAP) for sharing their resources and wisdom.

This has been my fourth writing project working with Cindy Bunch. You've been a terrific editor. Thank you for believing in me.

Thanks to the anonymous readers who critiqued a very long, redundant and unfocused manuscript. They wrote pages of incredibly helpful notes that I treated like gold in my editing phase.

Speaking of gold, Margaret and our son Sam are my Fort Knox. You two make my life rich.

Lastly, thanks to Britt Beckelhymer and Megan Walker, managers at the Panera Bread Company in Atlanta where most of the book was written. They graciously let me stay for four hours at a time in "my booth" and even checked in on me to encourage me. I hope there will be a Panera in heaven. Their hazelnut blend coffee and Asiago cheese bagels are celestial.

All of the episodes recounted are true, but some names have been changed to honor privacy.

Though the terms "Asian Pacific American" and "Asian Pacific Islander" are growing in use and may soon become our accepted moniker, I use "Asian American" to minimize confusion for those still adjusting to the current term.

INTRODUCTION

All for You, Jack Zogg

I was only ten but I would have jumped off any cliff for Jack Zogg.

Age ten, baseball was my world, the Robins my team and Jack my manager. It just didn't get any better. We had Mark Taku and Johnny Lobrovich pitching, the Dow brothers, Tommy and Jim, anchoring the infield at first and shortstop, and Roland Martin on the hot corner. Being one of three ten-year-olds in the "majors" (most were in the minor league, a few stragglers were in PeeWees), I was content for a few innings a game in right field.

That year's Campbell Little League All-Star team, with Mark and Johnny as two of its best pitchers and Jack as its coach, went all the way to Williamsport, Pennsylvania, and won the 1962 Little League World Series. Youth baseball on the west side of San Jose was no small deal and Jack was, if not king, at least crown prince. To be a Robin was like being a Jet or Shark in *West Side Story*. There was great pride in playing for Jack Zogg.

Jack was a handsome, rugged and dashing bachelor. He did outside work, something like surveying. He usually came to practice wearing blue jeans, a somewhat white T-shirt and mud-caked boots and always his blue cap with the white "R." Jack had coached the Robins for so long, they were synonymous and interchangeable: Jack/Robins, Robins/Jack. Everyone knew.

I looked around the league at the other coaches. All but Jack had sons playing on their teams. He was simply there because he loved baseball and wanted to invest his off-hours in boys who shared his love. Nothing else obligated him to be there. That impressed me. Jack got us to play as a team committed to winning but never at the expense of experiencing the sheer joy of playing baseball. His practices were as good as playing in the games he managed. While pitching batting practice, he'd stop to point out a flaw in our swing ("Don't drop the left elbow, Rollo!"). If we executed well, his "Nice stroke, Paulie, you kept your head on the ball" would motivate us for the next pitch. Developing our skills, teaching us to play as a true team and helping us love and respect the game of baseball were his passions.

I managed my own Little League team in my early twenties, the South Pasadena Giants. "What would Jack do now?" became my silent mantra. When a sobbing ten-year-old Mark Kranwinkle struck out to end a game, I took him for a walk around the field to convince him he didn't lose the game all by himself—and I pictured Jack with his arm around my shoulder after one of my blunders. When the baseball bug bit me again at age forty-three, the fundamentals he taught me thirty-plus years earlier quickly came back to me as an outfielder in Atlanta's Men's Senior Baseball League.

Jack did for me what neither teacher nor parent was able to do at the time. He somehow spoke into the deepest part of my being: *Paulie, you can do it.*

He believed in me far more than I could. The next year, I was spanked by my sixth-grade teacher in front of the whole school for bad behavior. A few hours later, Jack was working hard to bring out the best in me during practice.

In a game that year, an opposing hitter lifted a blooper between second baseman Marty Maybie and me in right. I charged full blast, figuring it was mine. Marty, thinking it was his, backpedaled hard. He was built like a brick and I was no thin, flexible straw. We crashed, both bodies flying in opposite directions.

Somehow I held onto the ball. Jack rushed onto the field and told the others to back away and give me air. The impact had knocked me out. Jack repeatedly picked me up by my belt, dropped me down, and pulled me up to bring me back to consciousness. When I came to, I smiled up at Jack. That catch was for him.

We didn't win the league championship that year. I think we came in second, but it wasn't for lack of effort or not knowing our goal to win it all.

The next year, the league expanded and each existing team was allowed only two holdovers from the previous year. Jack had to choose between Wayne Payton, Rob McClelland and me. Wayne, the best pitcher in the league, was a given. Rob and I were pretty even. I couldn't imagine not playing for the Robins my last season. I had played two seasons for the Robins, Rob only one, so I figured I had a slight edge.

On draft day, Jack chose Rob and my name went in the draft pool. Death couldn't have felt any worse. The new Knights of Pythias took me with the first pick but that was no consolation. I sat alone against the outfield fence, head in my glove, and wept. Even Cathy McLain, cutest blonde at school, tried to console me but couldn't. I was no longer one of Jack's boys.

About twenty-five years later, I was visiting my hometown. I had been reflecting on who had impacted my life growing up. I decided to drop by the old field to see if I could find Jack. I ran into Bob Holman, still the league president. The park was named after him; he still seemed to live there. I guess my looks hadn't changed much from age twelve to thirty-seven; he remembered me and even what position I played. I told him why I was looking for Jack and he insisted I give him a call. "He'll want to hear from you, Paulie."

There was only one Jack Zogg in the San Jose phone book. He quickly remembered me. "Jack, I just had to tell you how great it was to play for you," I said. "I know I was a pretty average player but you brought out the best in me. I liked baseball but playing for you made me love the game. You made me believe I could make the play. Thank you."

We didn't talk long but my mission had been accomplished.

Titling this book *Jack Zogg's Guide to Asian American Leadership* would undoubtedly have left many readers puzzled and few books purchased. But I could have because Jack Zogg's leadership is imprinted on me for life. Like Jack, I try to find what motivates an individual to excel and then tap into it. Like Jack, I don't just invest myself in the best and the brightest. I look for that ten-year-old with passion and who has that little spark in their eye that says, "Teach me, train me." Like Jack, I have big goals and dreams. Like

Throughout this book, I will refer primarily to four unique cultures. A word of explanation here might be helpful:

Asian *culture refers to the cultures found in Asian countries.*

Asian American culture *refers to the culture of those of Asian descent living in the United States.*

Western culture *refers to the culture of those from European countries.*

Multiethnic culture *or* multiethnicity *refers to the culture when several ethnicities come together in the marketplace or in social or religious gatherings.*

These are not perfect categories or definitions, but they will give a general sense of major sociological groupings.

Two other terms are also used repeatedly:

Assimilation *includes identification with the majority white culture; integration into schools, workplace, social groupings; and marital assimilation (when married to non-Asians).*

Ethnic identity *focuses on the retention of ethnic ways.*

Jack, when someone is flat on their back, I get hands-on to get them back onto their feet.

Jack Zogg led well. It took me a while to find my own "leadership legs" but when I did, I tried to lead like Jack.

On behalf of Jack and your elders, may I invite you to lead?

YOUNG ASIAN AMERICANS: AN AMAZING GENERATION

In my thirty years of ministry in a parachurch movement and in local churches, the first twenty-four were focused on working with the wide spectrum of students found on college campuses. Because nineteen of those twenty-four years were on campuses in the Southeast, I mainly worked with white and African American students. During the first twenty-two of those thirty years, I was active in three churches that were primarily white.

The last six years of ministry have focused on Asian American university students and young adults around the country. In short, you blow me away. You bring a unique combination of qualities to the kingdom table that are needed by the church, Asian American or otherwise:

- strong family backgrounds: while much is said about Asian American parents being domineering and sometimes controlling of their children, they tend to give far more attention to their children than their non-Asian American counterparts

- for many, churched backgrounds: you grew up valuing worship, spiritual disciplines, fellowship and missions; church is part of your DNA

- because of your strong church upbringing, you care deeply about your home churches

- some helpful Confucian-based values that are consistent with biblical qualities, like respect for elders, reflection and solitude, tending to other's needs before one's own, the value of being in community, hospitality, looking out for younger siblings

- baseball caps and hip-hop fashion aside, you tend to be more aligned with the baby boomer generation and less "Gen-Xish" in your orientation and values than your white friends, making you more appealing receivers of the generational leadership baton

- highly educated: one of every seven Asian Americans twenty-five and older have advanced degrees—that adds up to one million of you; 78 percent of the 1999 high school graduating class of Asian Americans went right into college—the highest proportion of any race group

- you're graduating in record numbers from our colleges—dynamic, talented, winsome Asian Americans, eager to see your potential tapped and developed. *Not when you are thirty-five or forty, but now.* If we don't affirm, develop and train you *now*, you're likely long gone. You will find a niche of serving and leading somewhere and it may be outside of the church.

My family worships at Atlanta Chinese Christian Church. I have an informal consulting/training role with the young adult fellowship leaders, an impressive array of gifted, teachable folks in their twenties and early thirties. I'm amazed at their willingness to work with our children and youth. They are also hungry to be mentored and trained for more leadership in the church. Michael and Veleda, Patrick, Jeffrey, Jennifer and Brian, Jeff, Eping, James and Jenny, Charlene—it's an all-star team.

AN INVITATION TO LEAD

My hope is this book will help equip and guide emerging leaders in Asian American churches and college fellowships, especially those in their twenties to mid-thirties.

The first section, "On Being a Leader," encourages you to start your journey as a leader or to stay on it if you are well on your way. The second section takes a different turn; "Developing and Deploying Asian American Leaders" addresses those who have responsibility for Asian American leaders. It seeks to give these people the big picture of Asian America and how to be helpful supervisors and mentors for Asian Americans.

Oswald Chambers wrote in *My Utmost for His Highest*, "One individual life may be of priceless value to God's purposes and yours may be that life."

Let's agree but change it a bit: "One emerging generation may be of priceless value to God's purposes and yours may be that generation."

ON BEING A LEADER

1 BUILDING THE SPIRITUAL FOUNDATIONS OF AN ASIAN AMERICAN LEADER

I am a leader but I was not born to lead. Let me explain.

Dad met Mom in 1945, just hours before he left Minneapolis for basic training in the Army at the Presidio in Monterey, California. His college plans back when he was eighteen had been postponed when he was sent to an internment camp for Japanese Americans in Amache, Colorado, in 1942. When he was released in 1944, he was more than ready to get on with his education. He had hopes of earning a Ph.D.

Because his family lost nearly everything when they were sent to "camp," Dad didn't have the means to attend college. He joined the Army in 1945 to take advantage of the G.I. Bill that provided education for military veterans.

Dad met Mom at the Episcopal Center at the University of Minnesota in Minneapolis. The center had been transformed into a halfway house for Japanese American internees, giving them a place to live as they got their feet back on the ground. Mom's parents served as the houseparents.

It was pretty much love at first sight, and Mom and Dad married in 1946. My sister was born in 1948 and I came along in 1951. Mom and Dad were deeply in love with each other and they loved Pam and me. If television needed an Asian American Cosby family, we were it.

At least we were until the car accident in 1953. The day after Mom's twenty-ninth birthday, we were on our way to a Japanese American community picnic in northern California when the drunk driver of a truck crossed over the line and hit us head-on.

Mom's last act was one of love for her family. I was in her arms. This was long before the advent of seatbelts. When she saw the truck veering into our lane, she threw me to the floorboard, a split second before she flew out the front windshield. She was killed immediately.

Dad was also pronounced dead, but clung to life and went into a coma. All his front teeth were knocked out and his face rearranged. He came out of the coma a few days later. Pam and I were also severely injured. None of us could attend Mom's funeral. Dad's plastic surgeon did such an outstanding job they became business partners and friends for life.

Dad remarried in 1954 and by 1959 we were a family of seven. For all of my growing-up years, we all acted like Mom never really existed. Her name never came up in dinner conversations or at Tokunaga gatherings. Yes, she gave birth to Pam and me, but our stepmom became Mom.

Looking back on my childhood and adolescence, the major theme was—I don't know a more polite way to put it—I was angry as hell. I often fought with Mom, who not only had Pam and me to raise but also three children of her own.

I knew I couldn't strike her, so I came up with a clever way to retaliate. After one of our tangles, I went out to the back patio. I took off my eyeglasses, which had glass lenses at least ten inches thick, and threw them with all my might onto the concrete. The plastic frames broke and the lenses shattered into dozens of pieces. I felt so good, until after the third pair when Mom said, "The next one you pay for."

My parents were bewildered and didn't know what to do with me. In fifth grade, they threatened to send me to military school if I didn't straighten up. My teachers threw up their hands, saying, "We don't know if we should skip Paul a grade because of his intelligence or send him back a grade because of his awful behavior." Perplexed, they did neither and braced themselves for my wildly erratic and often damaging behavior.

My most shameful and humiliating episode of childhood came in sixth grade. It was a bad year for me. For my parent-teacher conference report that spring, Mr. Benson, my teacher, wrote, "Socializing interferes with classroom activities. Not used to dealing with constructive criticism. Refuses to speak when there is a behavior difficulty. Whining and lazy about some things."

During lunch hour that year, Mr. Benson was taking his turn as lunch cop in the cafeteria. I was just being myself but one of my antics was the last straw for him. He yanked me out of my seat and dragged me by the collar onto the cafeteria stage. He sat down and in front of the entire school, kindergarten through sixth grade, put me across his knee and spanked me over and over.

It was hard enough that Margie Pack, the girl I really wanted to like me, watched. Much worse was knowing that my younger siblings, kindergartner Howard and first-grader Susan, were watching their older brother— *Number One Son, Role Model*—being thrashed before three hundred kids. Kirk Gatsby immediately became my best friend when he loaned me his baseball glove, allowing me to walk out with my face buried in it so no one could see my tears and humiliation.

Sixth grade was bad, but things got worse in seventh and eighth. Finally, my freshman year, in the aftermath of another fight with my stepmom, I started the homeless movement in California. I ran away from home. I lived in the back yard of a vacant house four doors down. Pam sneaked me food and clean clothes. I went to school trying to act normal. At night, I wandered the streets with a heart that had been ripped apart and was bleeding badly. After a week, Mom came to school and pulled me out of class. We struck détente and I went home.

I was like Dr. Jekyll and Mr. Hyde throughout high school. While I was senior class president, nearly everything I owned I had stolen. As I was being applauded for my performances in school plays, I came close to suicide because my public and private lives were two people in one body. The charade was driving me crazy.

NEW LIFE, OLD ISSUES

I came to faith in Jesus during my senior year in high school. I clearly needed a savior. I went away to college and grew like a spiritual weed. I became one of those laid-back Californian Jesus freaks. I thought everything was cool. I definitely thought I was cool.

Then I got married.

When Margaret and I went through premarital counseling, we took one of those how-are-they-going-to-get-along psychological tests. On the section that told us if we were mellow, angry or somewhere in-between, I redlined on anger. I was totally shocked. I hadn't thrown my glasses in years. I thought Jesus had swapped out my anger for faith, hope and love. It didn't shock Margaret, however. She had seen glimpses of it during our long-distance courtship.

I had brought my childhood anger into our marriage. I watched it nearly destroy my relationship with Margaret. She struggled with depression our first few years of marriage. She sought out a Christian counselor, and after nearly a year of counseling she encouraged me to join her to discuss issues that affected our marriage.

After several sessions, our counselor invited me to come on my own. I did so for a year and a half. I began to see my anger more clearly and how destructive it was. But then counseling became too threatening. The changes it conjured up seemed impossible. It was easier to live trying to keep my anger in check than to get to the root of it. I wasn't sure what was in Pandora's box and I was too scared to open it to find out.

In 1988, I was promoted and we moved to Atlanta. A new city, a new job and I thought a new chapter in my life. But the same old anger moved with me. Margaret started counseling again. This time, it took me less time to agree to marriage counseling. I saw how my anger affected those closest to me: Margaret, our son Sam and the six people I supervised. They all deserved better.

Counseling was exhausting. For several years, when we addressed very difficult parts of my behavior, I would leave therapy and go to a nearby mall. With glazed eyes and numb body, I wandered around the mall like a zombie. I kept my supervisor up-to-date on how I was doing. Occasionally, after therapy, I would tell him, only half in jest, that I was thinking of driving across that double yellow line. He would encourage me not to, and only half in jest told me to stay out of tall buildings with windows that opened.

At one critical juncture when therapy was extremely difficult, I told Margaret and Penny, our therapist, "I'm satisfied with who I am. I don't think I'm that bad of a person. There are far worse people out there than me." That said, I had put down an important stake. I was saying, "I can't take any more of this. I don't want to change anymore. I don't think I can. It's too hard. Take me as I am or don't take me at all."

In the following weeks, I realized that I had set myself on a disaster course. Heading down that road meant I would probably would lose everything that mattered most to me: my wife, my son, my ministry. My life. I quickly got off that path.

REDISCOVERING MY ROOTS

Sometime later, in one of my solo therapy sessions, Penny said, "Paul, tell me about your life from the beginning."

I could hear her clock registering cha-ching cha-ching, so I started giving the abridged version. "I was born to . . . in a log cabin without cable TV . . . we didn't have much . . . Mom died when I was eighteen months old . . . Dad remarried . . . they had three kids, now we were five . . ."

"Whoa, Paul, whoa," Penny said. "Let's back up. Your mom died when you were eighteen months old? How did that happen? What was your mom like?"

I didn't have much to say since no one in the Tokunaga family had told me anything. Everyone was afraid to bring it up in deference to my dad.

"Can you find out about your mom?" Penny asked. "What she was like as a person, as a mother?"

So at age forty-two, I started to get to know Mom for the first time. I asked her older sister, my Auntie Sachi, if she had any pictures of Mom, if she would tell me stories about her, anything. She got her younger brother to send me an incredible panorama picture of Mom's funeral at the Marysville Buddhist Temple, the largest funeral ever held in that small northern California town. She called Lucy Brewer and asked her if she had anything to send me.

Lucy Brewer's name meant nothing to me until I received a package from her. Enclosed was a book, one of those blank journals. What would a white woman know about my mother? On the first page she inscribed, "My Friend Miyo," then she penned seventeen pages of memories of Mom. They had met when Mom was released from the Minidoka, Idaho, internment camp in 1944 and moved to Kansas City, then on to Minneapolis. When Mom got a job at the Young Quinlan department store downtown, Lucy was assigned to train her. "I still remember what she was wearing [that first day]. A very pretty white dressy blouse with a red wool pleated skirt. Wow!"

They became fast friends. "She was sweet, charming, ever so polite and soon won everyone's heart." Lucy would often take her home to the family farm in Minnesota. Frequently, Mom, Lucy and Gloria, another white friend, would go out in Minneapolis. "Many times when we would be out together, people would give us really dirty looks and say things because we were hanging around 'that Jap.'"

In this book of memories, Lucy taped in things I had never seen: Mom and Dad's wedding invitation, my birth announcement, and letters from Mom to Lucy. I had never thought of it before but I had never seen her handwriting. I can't describe the emotions as I read her words about her precious baby—Paul.

Clearly, God had protected these mementos. I called Lucy to thank her. I had to know why she had kept them for over forty years. "Paul, your mom was special to me," she said. "I just figured someday, someone would want them. I've just waited for that time to come."

Mom—who had been just a name—was coming into focus. I needed to know more so I went to the one who knew her best and loved her most. Dad. Penny discouraged me from asking him. "It's too painful for him, Paul."

But I felt I would be going behind his back, asking my relatives without giving him a chance to give me his memories of Mom. I wrote him a simple note, "Dad, I am in therapy with a psychiatrist. I'm dealing with some difficult issues in my life. Part of the process is trying to recall things from my earliest years. I was wondering if you could tell me about Mom—what she was like, how she was as a mother to Pam and me. If you aren't able to do this, that's okay, I certainly understand. Thanks. Love, Paul."

I took a deep breath, prayed and stuck it in the mailbox. A week later I received his response. I was returning from a trip and Margaret had read it and prepared me for it. "You'd better sit down," she said.

Dad had written three single-spaced typewritten pages. His recollections about Mom poured out, as if he had been wearing a "Push Me" button for forty years and everyone had been afraid to. Now that the button had been pushed, incredibly vivid memories gushed forth.

Most of them are too private to share publicly, but through his words, I saw Mom clearly for the first time. A few snippets I can share:

"She liked people; made good friends. This could be the trait you inherited, Paul."

"To this day, I can never get over Miyo's tragic death. She had so much to live for and just when things started to look up for us, she left us."

"She was a tremendous mother to you and Pam. She raised you two well even though it was for a very short time. She was very happy to have a daughter and a son."

I was discovering she had a charming, vivacious personality. People loved being around her. She was the life of any party. A friend of hers put it this way, "When Miyo entered a room, she would light it up with laughter." Mom was a passionate person. She craved time with her close friends and would scold them for not coming to see her.

She adored Pam and me. Along with Dad, we were the lights of her life, the apples of her eye. We were her everything and more. Lucy had sent me pictures of Mom and Dad—at a coffee shop, on the dance floor, at the beach—gazing into each other's eyes. And pictures of her with Pam and me—the same loving gaze.

One of Mom's sisters-in-law gave me a letter written by Mom to her in January of 1953, two months before the accident:

Our menace [that would be me, sixteen months old] is up from his nap. Honestly, if he doesn't wear me to a frazzle. He's ten times more work than Pam was and ten times more active. Today he has a black eye from climbing the high chair—the lid fell on his eye. You'd think he'd stay away after that but two minutes later, he's climbing it again. Yesterday he found Pam's treasured Mountain Bar candy she's been saving for after dinner and he ate it all up sitting in the closet. First time he's had candy and was he going to town.

Last night I gave him a bath and put his sleepers on and he jumped off

the bed—ran into the bathroom and climbed into the bathtub with Pam—
clothes and all. And then Kats [my dad] can't understand why I don't want
another baby. That's just an example of the many things he does all day long
but he sure is a happy kid, laughing and smiling all day—that's when he's
not fighting with Pam. You're lucky you have another girl.

On top of that he weighs 28 lbs.—breaks my back, he's always on it,
thinks I'm a horse I guess because 'cuz every time he gets on my back he
has to have his gun and wants me to gallop.

Through letters and conversations with relatives, I continued to get to
know her and understand her. I read a book that described a baby's first
twelve months of life. Each chapter covered a month, describing the baby's world, what they could take in and comprehend. I found the follow-
up volume that described the second twelve months. By the time I hit
month eighteen—my age when she died—I was overwhelmed with how
much babies take in, especially from their chief nurturer. Theirs is an especially strong, bonding and important relationship.

When I put together these books with the memories of friends and relatives, it was clearer than crystal: Mom had deeply shaped me with her
love and care.

As this knowledge started sinking in, I was swept away by being loved
by this incredible woman who brought me into this world, gave her life
to me and in the end, quite literally gave her life for me. I am Miyo
Tokunaga's son. I was loved and nurtured in ways that I carry to this day.
(I am also fortunate to have a stepmom who treats me like her own and
loves me deeply, as I now do her.)

At fifty-one, I am still the kid who climbs the high chair, gets a black
eye and gets up again. I persevere. I am a survivor. I still dive into bath-
tubs fully clothed, in a manner of speaking. I take calculated risks (bath-
tubs, not the Atlantic Ocean!). I still look for the chocolate hidden in dark
closets, literally. No longer 28 lbs., I still have a cowboy inside of me,
ready to gallop for the right cause or reason.

Mom was such a nurturer and protector for me that these and other
early patterns locked in those first eighteen months and never left me.
Now I know: I am Miyo Tokunaga's son through and through.

But it was a bittersweet gaining of knowledge. She was dead. I only had her as my mother for eighteen months. She abandoned me. Of course it wasn't intentional. Leaving Pam and me motherless and Dad a widower wasn't her choice. Still, I felt abandoned.

And I feel abandoned. When an aunt or uncle reminisces on how great Miyo was, a lance pierces my heart. How might my life have been different had I been raised by her? Would I be a more secure person, especially with women I am close to? Would I not wonder if they might abandon me?

Just this year, after having lunch with Auntie Sachi, where we talked at length about Mom, I was overwhelmed with a sense of loss. I sat alone in my rental car on a side street in Los Angeles, sobbing. "Why did you have to go? I miss you so much."

This is the point where well-intentioned people would want to grip my shoulder and share Romans 8:28 with me: "And we know that in all things God works for the good of those who love him, who have been called according to his purpose." I appreciate their thoughtfulness.

How we translate that verse and apply it to life's difficult situations means everything. If we take it to mean, "Bad things happen to good people and if you wait long enough or pray hard enough this bad thing will start looking good to you" then God is a powerless, deistic spin doctor who can only change our perspective, not our lives. Spiritually, I'd rather go back to the faith of my youth—Buddhism—than follow a God who deceives. The Buddha never claimed god status; what you see is what you get.

What God *does* promise in that verse is that out of all things—great or awful—he is right there in the trenches with us, working for our good. He doesn't change the past. He doesn't spare us the sufferings common to all sons and daughters of Adam. What we can take to the bank is that he is in this fray with us and nothing can separate him from those whom he loves. That's his promise. I can play ball with a God like that.

Losing Mom was the singular tragedy of my life. Not everyone has lost a parent, though all of us will someday. All of us, I venture, do have a tragedy, heartache or deep secret that we prefer to ignore or hide. We press on. What good can come of lifting the cover and exposing our dark stuff to the light?

I'm convinced "meeting Mom" in my forties has made me a better leader and person. When someone loses a loved one, in my hug or condolence card comes not just sympathy but empathy. Lately I've noticed how reading of family tragedies in the newspaper provokes a jab in my heart. Up to a few years ago, I felt nothing for the pained stranger. Though I have never been good at it, I am getting better at what Paul describes in 2 Corinthians 1:3-5:

> Praise be to the God and Father of our Lord Jesus Christ, the Father of compassion and the God of all comfort, who comforts us in all our troubles, so that we can comfort those in any trouble with the comfort we ourselves have received from God. For just as the sufferings of Christ flow over into our lives, so also through Christ our comfort overflows.

The word Paul uses for comfort translates best as "walking alongside." Author Earl Palmer describes it as someone who is walking solo on a long journey when a friend comes alongside and walks the rest of the journey with her. Understanding this in my life helps me walk alongside and bring some comfort to those who have experienced a major loss in their life. I've been there.

Especially when working with young Asian Americans, I learn all I can about how they were brought up and what their relationships with family members were like. As we listen well, we might free up people to bring to the light issues that have been quashed and submerged for years.

The list of benefits goes on. Forgiving Mom for abandoning Pam and me helps me forgive those guilty of smaller abandonments. I am more empathic toward others who are in pain. When I meet the parent of someone I know well, I delight in seeing in them the qualities I love in their child.

OWNING OUR SOVEREIGN FOUNDATIONS

The people whom we lead deserve only the very best we have to offer. We bring not just our skills but also our character and the stuff that resides in our heart. Leaders can crush and destroy. We've seen it, maybe on the receiving end. Leaders can also bring life and hope. Like the paramedic who brings one back from near death, our leadership, like Jack Zogg's in my life, helps some to shout *I can do this, I really can!* And by golly, they sometimes do.

Leaders of that caliber didn't get it from an MBA program alone or even from years of experience. Training and on-the-job know-how are important but we all know educated, experienced leaders who are mediocre. We don't want to join their ranks so we ask, "What else?"

What else does it take to be the truly exceptional leader? How do we call forth from people stuff they didn't even know was there? How do we enable others to succeed, with lines forming outside our doors?

It begins with a life before God. The exceptional leader opens up every door into her life and says, "Come, Lord Jesus. There's work to be done. I invite you as the Great Excavator to mine and extract the bad coal so I might serve and lead others well."

The sign on one of those doors reads "Sovereign Foundations."

Fuller Theological Seminary professor Robert Clinton, in his important book *The Making of a Leader*, outlines five phases of a leader's life: sovereign foundations, inner-life growth, ministry maturing, life maturing, convergence.

> In this [first] sovereign foundations phase, God providentially works through family, environment and historical events. You might find it hard to believe that God was working through your family or your environment, especially if these were not godly influences, but he was. Keep in mind that it is often difficult to see the importance of all these items until later phases.
>
> God is developing the leader by laying foundations in his (her) life. This operation is sovereign. The potential leader has little control over what happens in this phase. His primary lesson is to learn to respond positively and take advantage of what God has laid in these foundations.[1]

Leaders by nature are forward-looking and we need to be. However, it's easy to overlook the significance of our past and how parts of it may directly and powerfully influence how we lead now and later. If I were talking with you about these things, I would show you a few of Mom's letters and some family pictures, and then ask, "What in your past needs to face the light?"

As Clinton says, "Keep in mind that it is often difficult to see the importance of all these items until later phases."[2]

Being Asian American doesn't make it easier to pull the cover off previously hidden things. We are simply the best when it comes to guarding family secrets. Exposing them risks shaming family members. Our loyalty gets questioned. If it involves a parent or older sibling, we are challenging hierarchy. We just don't go there and still retain our place in the family order. It's much easier to "go Japanese" with their guiding principle of *shikata ga nai*: "It cannot be helped, it has to be."

Intrinsically, we tend not to fight the system. We give in to "Asian fatalism." When we do give in, we rob God of a chance to work a miracle or two. We think that dying with angst, a hard heart and bitterness is far less painful.

SOVEREIGN FOUNDATIONS AND BEING A LEADER

What do our sovereign foundations have to do with leadership? Nothing less than everything. My past directly impacted what kind of leader I was becoming. I began to see that I would never lead well until some of my damaged past was healed. I needed to forgive some key people in my life whom I felt had let me down. Dealing head-on with this sovereign foundation is reaping fruit in my life and ministry.

Some of us, maybe most of us, have episodes or relationships from the past that either freeze us in our tracks or so overwhelm us with guilt or shame that we hit the "delete" button whenever it comes up on the screen of our minds. I know I did this with Mom. It was easier to forget that she was part of my life than to admit how mad I was that she had abandoned me.

Don't hit the delete button on those things from the past that keep coming up on the screen of your mind. Don't even hit the "page down" button when something hits the screen that horrifies you. The God who owns the book that contains "all the days that were formed for me, when none of them as yet existed," is never surprised or caught off-guard. He is the one who comforts us in all our troubles.

Dealing with our deep secrets and wounds will liberate us to become better leaders. It won't be easy and it may take years or even decades of exploration and hard work. There may be valleys where our leadership suffers for a season. Mine did. But seasons do end and what emerges is a healthier leader with much more to offer their followers.

Around the time I was getting to know Mom via letters and photographs, I was serving as regional director for InterVarsity Christian Fellowship in the Southeastern United States. I had appointed Paul Litten to be the area director for our ministry in South Florida. At the end of his first year, we reviewed and evaluated the year. During such evaluations, I always give those I supervise the opportunity to critique my supervision of them and to offer input that might make me a better boss.

Paul, always candid and honest, told me, "I keep waiting for you to blow up at me. Others told me to watch out when you do, it isn't pretty, but you haven't done it yet."

What may have seemed minor to Paul was gargantuan to me. I walked away from that appointment full of praise and gratitude. God was healing me.

UNDERSTANDING OUR ASIAN DNA

Along with owning our sovereign foundations, like I had to with my birth mother, I see two other essential components for Asian American leaders as we develop our spiritual lives. First, believe God made no mistakes when he made us. Second, have an awareness of our unique "Asian DNA," which can both undercut and enhance our spiritual development.

GOD DOESN'T MAKE MISTAKES

David affirms in Psalm 139 how God had his creative hand upon him. Can we also say the same for ourselves? What questions does this text raise for us? Here are a few of mine from over the years, with some personal reflections.

For it was you who formed my inward parts.

"Lord, did you mean for my eyes to be so slanted, narrow and brown, not blue? My nose so flat? My hair jet black and so straight? Speaking of hair, couldn't you have put just a little on my chest? And another foot in height sure would have helped my chances for the NBA."

You knit me together in my mother's womb.

"Knitting is painstakingly slow. Every stitch is deliberate and the color of each skein critical. Were you that careful when you formed me?"

I praise you, for I am fearfully and wonderfully made.

"Wonderfully, Lord? Michael Jordan, maybe. Catherine Zeta-Jones, perhaps. Paul Tokunaga? Me, a wonder?"

Wonderful are your works;
that I know very well.

"Okay, okay, you made your point."

My frame was not hidden from you,
when I was being made in secret,
intricately woven in the depths of the earth.

"Intricately woven! There you go with that knitting thing again. God, could it actually be that of all the centuries for me to be born in, you chose the twentieth? Of all nationalities I could have been, you chose Japanese? Of all possible mothers I could have had you chose Miyo Kumagai Tokunaga for me? Of all places, Marysville, California?"

Your eyes beheld my unformed substance.

"Before I was a thought in Katsumi and Miyo's minds, you had been thinking about me. Not just thinking of me, you looked at me. Before my fingers became fingers and elbows became elbows, you were checking me out, eager to create another masterpiece."

In your book were written
all the days that were formed for me,
when none of them as yet existed.

"September 3, 1951; March 28, 1953; September 11, 1954; December 25, 1968; August 27, 1977; December 26, 1983—there they were, in your own handwriting! You weren't surprised when I was born, when Mom was killed, when Dad remarried, when I accepted Christ, when Margaret and I married, when Sam was born. You knew, didn't you, all the time?"

How do *you* read Psalm 139:13-16? Do you sometimes feel like a mistake? Do you wonder if God's hard drive locked up when your name was coming up? Or do you believe you are one of God's wonderful works? Do you *feel* fearfully and wonderfully made?

These are critical questions to answer. How we answer them helps us decide whether we can fully give the rest of our lives to God. Is the God of our tomorrow also the God of our yesterday?

For me, personalizing Psalm 139 means asking myself pointed questions: Did God have a purpose in making me Japanese American? Did God have a reason for putting me in family of Katsumi and Miyo Tokunaga? Was he in control or on lunch break when twenty-six of my relatives—parents, grandparents, aunts, uncles, cousins—were put in internment camps during World War II? Did God make a giant computer error when he put me in a family that was Buddhist for generations?

Then there's the hardest question of all: Did God have a plan for my good when my mother was killed in that head-on collision, leaving my sister and me without an incredibly nurturing mother and my father without the love of his life?

All the days ordained for me were written in the book before one of them came to be.

"Even March 28, 1953, Lord, on that two-lane road outside of Marysville, California?"

How we read and understand Psalm 139:13-16 also directly impacts our spiritual lives. If the God of the universe takes that much interest in me, I must be incredibly important and valuable to him. I'm not just one of millions. For God, I'm one of one, a masterpiece, wonderfully made. Knowing and believing that, I can lead with God-inspired confidence. I don't have to lead others exactly like my leaders led me. How I lead will be unique because I am unique.

My son Sam had a great T-shirt and even had the audacity to wear it as a young teenager. On the front side: "Never before, never again." On the back: "I am a legend in the making!" Rarely has such solid theology made it onto a T-shirt. It's so true: never will there be one quite like each of us. Here's another great T-shirt idea, right from question one of the *Children's Catechism.*

On the front: "Who made you?"

On the back: "God."

ASIAN DNA

Old paint on canvas, as it ages, sometimes becomes transparent. When that happens, it is possible, in some pictures, to see the original lines: a tree will show through a woman's dress, a child makes way for a dog, a large boat is no longer on an open sea.[1]

Lillian Hellman wasn't thinking of Asian Americans when she wrote these opening lines in *Pentimento* but her imagery works. We *see*, in fact, we *are* the picture on top—a woman's dress, a child, a boat. Underneath are the nearly visible images that get clearer the longer and harder one stares. These are the forces that shape and mold us. Sometimes they aid us on our spiritual journey, other times they cut us off at the knees.

Another component of our spiritual development involves recognizing the main brushstrokes already on our canvas as an Asian American. This is our Asian deoxyribonucleic acid, the genetic material within us.

While they don't predetermine who we are or what we will become, our fingerprints as Asian Americans carry enough similar DNA molecules with the same sense strands that patterns emerge. To not acknowledge their place in our life and come to terms with how they impact our spiritual life would be to rob ourselves of going deeper with God.

I use the term DNA here more descriptively than scientifically. When I refer to our "Asian DNA," I mean those traits or qualities that seem to persist and be present in us as Asian Americans. For most Asian nationalities, especially those rooted in East Asia, five sense strands—Confucianism, shame, suffering, our families and liminality—stand out to me.

CONFUCIANISM

Koreans, Chinese and Japanese are Confucian-based people. The teachings of Confucius form the warp and woof of these cultures. While his imprint is also on Southeast and South Asian nationalities (such as Filipino, Cambodian, Vietnamese, Indian and Pakistani), they are not as steeped in and influenced by Confucianism as those with East Asian heritage.

For most Asian Americans, Confucianism is not a religion or even a philosophy to which we would intentionally devote ourselves. Rarely would we say "I'm a follower of Confucius" in the same way one might say "I follow Jesus." I've yet to see a "Confucius Loves Me" T-shirt. Rather, it permeates our social and family structures, much in the way Americans do not recite the Declaration of Independence but certainly have the values of the Declaration woven into the fabric of our society.

Confucius's *Lunyu* or *Analects*, considered to be the most reliable source of information about his life and teachings, were practical and ethical rather than religious. Confucius held that proper outward acts based on the five virtues of kindness, uprightness, decorum, wisdom and faithfulness constitute the whole of human duty. Reverence for parents, living and dead, was one of his key concepts.

The tenets of Confucianism center around the concepts of *jen* and *lĭ*. Jen is a combination of the characters for "human being" and for "two"; thus empathetic humanity should be at the foundation for human relations. Lĭ is a combination of morality and etiquette, custom and ritual.

> Confucius (K'ung Ch'iu or K'ung Fu-Tzu) was a teacher and philosopher, then later a government official, who lived in what is now the Shantung province of China during the latter part of the Zhou (or Chou) Dynasty from 551 to 479 B.C.
>
> Vice and corruption were rampant and Confucius used his position as minister of crime to bring remarkable reform. He felt strongly that rulers could be great only if their own lives were above reproach and guided by moral principles. He never claimed deity for himself and had little belief in the supernatural.

Lĭ   Rén

At the core of Confucian ethics is *rén*, variously translated as "love," "goodness," "humanity" and "human-heartedness." Also at the heart of his teaching was that successful individual human relations form the basis of society. To bring order to society, one must first bring order to the family, which will ultimately bring order to the community, which will then bring order to the government.

Some other strong values of Confucianism include parental authority and honor (known as "filial piety": children must honor and obey parents, putting their comfort, interest and wishes above their own), social hierarchy, male dominance, duty and obligation, and education. Some aspects of Confucian thought are quite compatible with Christianity.

- Like Confucianism, the Bible calls us to honor our parents (Lev 19:2-3; Deut 5:16; Prov 6:20-23; Eph 6:1).

- Like Confucianism, we are to put the desires of others above our own (Phil 2:3-4; 1 Cor 10:24).

- Like Confucianism, Christianity recognizes that when primary relationships are made right, the larger society is bettered (Mt 5:11-16).

But some aspects of Confucian thought clash with Christian faith. Some of it may be because of differing missions, some of it because of differing ideology. Confucianism can undermine spiritual development in at least three areas.

First, *Confucian ideology of women distorts the spiritual lives of both Asian American women and men.* In *Korean American Ministry,* In Sook Lee writes:

That [Korean] culture has consistently considered women inferior to men. Korean women were required to obey their fathers before marriage, their husbands after marriage, and their sons in old age. They early learned to be quiet, submissive, and obedient under all circumstances. Most of these restrictions were rooted in a Korean type of Confucian philosophy.[2]

Lee continues, "Confucian ideology relegated women to an inferior position and its leaders expended great effort to indoctrinate both sexes into supporting this social order."[3]

In *Asian American Dreams: The Emergence of an American People,* Helen Zia says, "Growing up female, I could see the Confucian order of the Three Obediences in action: the daughter obeys the father, the wife obeys the husband, and, eventually, the widow obeys the son. The Confucian tradition was obviously stacked against me, as a girl."[4]

Jesus would have taken Confucius to the woodshed over how he viewed women's place in their families. When his travels took him to the village of Bethany, a suburb of Jerusalem, Luke in his Gospel doesn't tell us, "Jesus called on Lazarus, who by the way, had two sisters, whose names, by the way, were Mary and what's her name? . . . uh, Martha, I think."

Rather, he emphasizes whose home it was: "As Jesus and his disciples were on their way, he came to a village where a woman named Martha opened her home to him" (Lk 10:38). Likewise, John levels the relational playing field: "Jesus loved Martha and her sister and Lazarus" (Jn 11:5).

When a belief system is deeply woven into the fabric of a culture, it affects all relationships. How can Asian American women approach God believing he wants the best for them when their own culture tells them that's not possible? How can we expect Asian American women to be fully functioning in the body of Christ—including exercising leadership gifts—if a still small voice keeps whispering, "What you have to offer is not as good as what a brother can bring"?

Frankly, I don't think it is women's sole responsibility to pull themselves up by their own bootstraps so they can be on equal footing with men. Asian American men, if not in this generation then in generations past, have perpetuated this inequality. Men must take responsibility for correcting our and our forefathers' wrongdoing.

As Asian American men we need to speak up on behalf of women in general and for specific women who are qualified to do certain tasks or fill specific roles. We need to be proactive and affirm, train and mentor the enormously gifted sisters in our midst. Woe to us and the body of Christ if men stay silent, thus assenting that we are better suited to follow Jesus and help his kingdom grow than are women.

As Asian American men we must also realize that such a distorted view of women hurts us. We, perhaps subconsciously, think we are better and deserve better. When we do that, we lose out on authentic partnership with women.

Second, *Confucius's extremely high view of education can undermine our desire to give Christ the preeminence in all we do.* Jung Young Lee writes in *Korean Preaching:*

> Education remains important to the Korean people. Americans often do not understand why Koreans are almost fanatical about education. Most Koreans want to attend the best schools and to attain the highest academic

degrees. Whenever they meet new people, they almost always ask: "What school did you go to? What schools do your children go to? What degrees have you received?" The Korean attitude toward education has been shaped by the teaching of Confucius, who was a great teacher.[5]

It is a subtle but strong message that roars in the ears of young Asian Americans. Eunice Park, a seventeen-year old columnist for *AsianWeek*, captures it well in her essay, "The SATs—1500 or Bust":

> We [Asian American teenagers] are more than the mere sum of our GPAs and SAT scores, which are only shallow measurements of our true selves. Too many don't realize this.
>
> I've already seen what can happen when students base their self-worth on a score: some stand up well in public but in private, they break down from all the pressure; others bare their shame, cry in class if they get a C on a test or miss a few points on a quiz.[6]

Asian American Christians are hardly immune from this pressure. At age seventeen or eighteen, it is very difficult to distinguish the voice of Confucius (with our parents singing lead) from the voice of Jesus. Jesus urges us to "love the Lord your God with all your mind," affirming the value of education but not as a means to either eternal life or earthly fulfillment. What at its core is a good thing can easily become an idol.

Third, *Confucianism overemphasizes some relationships to the exclusion of others*. Confucianism "is essentially a way of life governed by five relationships: between father and son, husband and wife, elder brother and younger brother, old and young, and the ruler and the ruled. These relationships are vertical and hierarchical in order. Among them, the relationship between the father and son is the key to all other relationships in life."[7] These five relationships are a start in the right direction but Confucius doesn't go far enough. Two obvious absences make such structure problematic for Christian faith.

One, women are only addressed if they are married. It raises the question, "Is the only place for a woman as a wife? What about women who sense God's call toward singleness?" The apostle Paul makes a compelling case for singleness (1 Cor 7:1). Confucius's "five relationships" also omit other family members like widows and divorcees who remain part of the family but could feel disenfranchised by this framework.

Two, if the father-son relationship is indeed the key to all other relationships *and* it is a hierarchical relationship, disagreement between the two generally results in father knows best. If in family life it is indeed the key relationship, then the other next four relationships are severely impacted by a poor father-son relationship.

Confucius was a good teacher, especially within the milieu of his time, but all good teachers have their blind spots and we must recognize he had plenty. There are times when he oversteps his boundaries as "wise uncle" and we must point him to the door as an unwelcome guest. How do you ask someone who has meant so much to you to please leave? Carefully and respectfully.

All cultures have their shakers and shapers. Ours is Confucius. As Christians, because we cannot serve two masters, we resist Lord Confucius and call only Jesus Lord.

SHAME

A second strand of our Asian DNA is shame. Simply put, Asian Americans are often affected more by shame, European Americans more by guilt, especially those brought up in the church.

European American morality finds its roots in Puritanism and in some biblical principles: the Ten Commandments, the Golden Rule, Proverbs and to a lesser degree the Sermon on the Mount. Throughout our country's history is the sense of "right is right and wrong is wrong." Up until recent years when a strong wave of relativism has threatened to wash away these standards, there has been a universal code of behavior, often referred to as "traditional values."

Stan Inouye, president of Iwa, a ministry to Asian Americans, writes, "While guilt occurs when an absolute standard is violated, shame occurs in a relational context."[8] Likewise, Tom Lin writes in *Losing Face and Finding Grace*, "Shame is interwoven into the fabric of the Asian family. Because our actions affect not only ourselves but entire generations of relatives and family, Asian Americans have a tough task ahead when they make mistakes and try to 'fix' it. Friends and family respond with 'You're not good enough!' or 'Why can't you do this as well as X does it?' or 'How could you shame us like that?' "[9]

GOOD SHAME, BAD SHAME

Ken Fong, pastor of Evergreen Baptist Church of Los Angeles, distinguishes between "healthy shame" and "toxic shame":

> *Healthy shame* is an intermittent, proper awareness of being a limited flawed human being. It leads to the acknowledgement of your need for help from a higher power. It is the source of creativity. It is the core of true spirituality. It is the healthy sense of sin that led many of the tax collectors and prostitutes to Jesus to receive forgiveness. *Asians being shame-based can be a real spiritual positive, not a negative, if it creates an ongoing need for Christ in us.*[10]

He references two biblical passages:

> Cover their faces with shame
> so that men will seek your name, O LORD. (Ps 83:16)

> If we claim to be without sin, we deceive ourselves and the truth is not in us. If we confess our sins, he is faithful and just and will forgive us our sins and purify us from all unrighteousness. If we claim we have not sinned, we make him out to be a liar and his word has no place in our lives. (1 Jn 1:8-10)

Toxic shame, on the other hand,

> is the dark feeling that you are flawed as a human being. In spite of your efforts to change, deep inside, it feels hopeless because you do not believe that genuine change is truly possible. After all, you did not just make a mistake, *you* are the mistake.

It is the reason we do not tell the truth about ourselves. It leads to portraying yourself to be a shameless person. It leads to spiritual bankruptcy that is camouflaged by practiced piety. It is the sin that kept the Pharisees and Sadducees from acknowledging their need for Jesus Christ. It is what prevents our churches from becoming true communities of grace, mercy, holiness and

SIGNS OF TOXIC SHAME IN US

What signs or hints inform us that we are struggling with toxic shame?

- *When someone tells us, "What a great job you did!" and we fire back, "No, no, I messed up with several parts of it."*

- *When our personal piety seems "too good to be true" to others because it probably is. There is so much shame that our "spiritual cosmetics" attempts to hide our true spiritual condition.*

- *When we are reluctant to talk candidly about our family, especially our relationship with our parents.*

- *When we have a hard time looking our spiritual leaders in the eye.*

- *When admittance to grad school at Cal or the University of Michigan or Columbia feels like a rejection of our personhood because Harvard and Stanford turned us down.*

- *When our public prayers are "I'm such a worm" offerings: filled with remorse, guilt, shame, and total unworthiness. Translation: "How can God stand me? He probably can't."*

- *When there is a reluctance to "own" our ethnicity. "I'm American (period, end of conversation, how's the weather?)."*

justice. Being driven by toxic shame is like having a hole in your soul.[11]

Being a leader starts with the recognition that you might have something to offer others. Shame shouts at me, "Who do you think you are, pal, that you think you could actually help that person grow and develop?"

Leadership demands from us the courage to make tough calls. It might be reprimanding someone or even firing them. It might mean being the stand-up person who rallies the troops to take the next hill. Shame shouts at me, "Sit down, worm! You're not worthy!"

Good leaders call out the best in others. That's impossible when one sincerely feels change is impossible—in themselves and in others. Spiritual leadership involves helping others go deeper with God. Shame mocks us, sneering, "Look at your own pitiful spiritual life. You missed two quiet times this week and you didn't share Christ with your coworker last week!" Shame, shame, shame on us!

More than anything, those of us from shame-based cultures need to know and experience God's unconditional, unearnable love. If shame causes you to feel you are a mistake, let these verses seep deeply into your marrow:

> Fear not, I have redeemed you; I have summoned you by name; you are mine. . . . Since you are precious and honored in my sight, and because I love you, I will give men in exchange for you and people in exchange for your life. (Is 43: 1-4)

> Those who look to him are radiant;
> their faces are never covered with shame. (Ps 34:5)

> Let us fix our eyes on Jesus, the author and perfecter of our faith, who for the joy set before him endured the cross, scorning its shame, and sat down at the right hand of the throne of God. (Heb 12:2)

The most powerful shame-killer is the cross on which Jesus chose to die. He "scorned" (or "disregarded," NRSV) the shame of the cross by voluntarily climbing it, taking upon himself the utter humiliation of the spiritual death we deserved.

SUFFERING

The suffering of our ancestors informs the present. Thus, the third strand of our Asian DNA is suffering.

For many South Asian nations, colonialism and civil unrest have been consistent themes. Indians struggled for several centuries as Britain's colony, finally gaining independence in 1947. Pakistan, along with its battles with India, has been plagued by constant civil unrest. Sri Lanka is beset by civil wars. Bangladesh fought for its independence from Pakistan, endured a major flood and internal strife.

The history of Cambodians has themes of fleeing extermination, starvation and governmental chaos. Pol Pot and the Khmer Rouge annihilated 1.7 million Cambodians, one-fifth of the entire country. Other Southeast Asian countries also suffered badly. Vietnam's history includes 1,400 years of Chinese rule and ninety years as a French colony. Today it is one of the few remaining Communist countries.

Koreans suffered at the hands of both the Chinese and Japanese. Korea has been a divided nation for over fifty years, separating friends and families. Andrew Sung Park in *Racial Conflict and Healing* writes, "Koreans believe themselves to be a *han*-ridden people, a people whose deep psychological wound has become their collective unconscious."[12]

"Han is a sense of unresolved resentment against injustice suffered, a sense of helplessness because of the overwhelming odds against, a feeling of acute pain of sorrow in one's guts and bowels making the whole body writhe and wiggle, and an obstinate urge to take 'revenge' and to right the wrong all these combined," says Korean theologian Young-Hak Hyun.[13]

Han is a Korean word but has equivalents in Chinese (*hen*—but much stronger and more negative—"to hate" and "to dislike") and Japanese (*kon*—"to bear a grudge" and "show resentment") and Vietnamese (*han*, similar to Korean *han*).

Japan suffered humiliation at the hands of the United States government in the mid-nineteenth century. Led by Commodore Matthew Perry, the United States pressured the highly seclusionary Japan into signing a "treaty of friendship" which opened the door for Western powers to undermine the authority of the *shogunate*, Japan's military-based leadership, and open trade with Japan on their own terms. About a hundred years later, Japan suffered not just humiliation but mass destruction at the hands of the United States with the atomic bombing of Hiroshima and Nagasaki.

For Chinese, suffering is the thickest skein in the tapestry of their long history. They have undergone not decades but centuries of famine and starvation. To this day, Chinese will greet each other not with a "Hello, how are you?" but "Have you eaten or not?" or "Have you had rice today?"

China also suffered at the hands of the Japanese. As much as Japan's government downplays it, Japanese soldiers did "rape Nanking" in the late 1930s during the Sino-Japanese War. Theodore H. White, the eminent historian, and Annalee Jacoby, write in *Thunder Out of China*, "Nanking, Chiang K'ai-shek's capital, fell on December 12, 1937, and an historic orgy of several weeks of rape, lust, and wanton murder followed."[14] Two hundred and fifty thousand Chinese were subjected to unwarranted abuse.

Japan's twentieth-century legacy of evil done to other Asian nations is shameful to all who carry Japanese blood. While I don't know how much responsibility I bear for the doings of forebears in another land, I do feel great shame and anguish. Every new story about Korean comfort women makes me want to apologize to my Korean American sisters. I am infuriated and saddened by new Japanese textbooks that express a lack of culpability for their twentieth-century atrocities and the refusal of Japan's leaders to own up to their wrongdoing. May God have mercy on them but also break through their hardened hearts to see and confess reality.

Japanese American suffering has been more recent. Prior to December 7, 1941, over 70 percent of all Japanese Americans lived in California. They "inherited much of the resentment and prejudice that had been directed against the Chinese."[15] Their phenomenal success as farmers increased animosity toward them.

When Pearl Harbor was bombed, it made it easy and convenient for Californians in particular to unleash their racism against Japanese Americans. President Franklin Roosevelt's infamous Executive Order 9066 called for the imprisonment of 120,000 Japanese Americans in "internment camps." Nearly all the fruit of a hard-working immigrant people rotted on the vine. Most lost almost everything.

In the camps, the centrality of nuclear families was threatened. Adolescents often ate with friends, not their families. There was a total lack of privacy in bathrooms. A single room averaging twenty feet by twenty feet was "home" for most families for two to three years. The camp experience bred a deep sense of shame: *We've done something wrong, we must have or our government wouldn't have done this to us, but what is it we have done wrong?*

Living behind barbed wire, with every move scrutinized by armed tower guards, germinated a lack of trust in authority figures. When the internees were released, the unspoken game plan was set in motion: be model citizens, don't protest anything, don't draw attention to yourself and blend in until you appear as white as your neighbor. *Shikata ga nai* ("it cannot be helped, it has to be") and *giri* ("doing what has to be done, quietly, with entirely stoic demeanor") were theme songs to get them through the nightmare.

Clearly, Asian history is laced with episodic suffering. But unlike the Western disposition toward it (suffering is abnormal, an aberration), Asians live with their histories blended with belief systems that see suffering as normative and expected. *Shikata ga nai* and *giri* ooze through our gritted teeth as we passively smile and accept our fate. It gets us through the day but leaves us with no hope for a better tomorrow.

SUFFERING LEADERS

I believe this theme of suffering for Asian Americans can affect our leadership in at least these ways:

- We will or ought to instinctively take the side of the underdog or those underrepresented or oppressed.

- We have opportunities to counter the long-term oppression of Asian women by giving them every opportunity to grow, develop, lead and succeed.

- Our suffering gives us a common heritage with other ethnic minorities. This should help us see them as comrades not competitors. Rather than being threatened by African Americans, their strengths complement our weaknesses and vice versa. We would make an awesome team. Rather than looking down on Hispanic Americans (especially Mexican Americans) as many of us are prone to do, our shared family values give us much in common.

- As God has "walked alongside" us in our travails, we have experienced his comfort. That comfort should equip us with "who's hurting?" antennae that lead us to anyone suffering so we might walk with them.

We *can* choose to respond in these ways if we first say no to being a victim who lives by the credo "poor, poor pitiful me."

OUR FAMILIES

A fourth strand of our Asian DNA is our families. Family means everything to Asian Americans. Wherever we go, we walk with our parents' shadow in front of us caused by their presence right behind us. Some call it a comforting presence; others a lurking presence, but always a presence.

Our parents can impact our spiritual lives in at least these four ways: First, *it's easy for us to mistake the voice of parents for God's voice.* Our uniquely high view of parental authority can something lull us to think it's his voice we are hearing when it is only our parents' and out of habit we obey it.

Second, *we carry the Confucian value of filial piety.* We believe that we children must unconditionally honor and obey parents, putting our parents' comfort, issues and wishes before our own.

Third, *our earthly fathers affect our view of the heavenly Father.* If your father is unapproachable, emotionally out of touch, seemingly unconcerned about everyday things in your life, it's very easy to see God the Father as not wanting an intimate relationship with you, one whom you can never really please and one who never hugs.

I was at a student conference when a college senior asked to meet with me. She quickly got to the point. She was going to be spending some time at home in the upcoming summer, and she feared being with her father. Growing up, he would often whip her to discipline her. This went on well into her teen years. I asked, "Are you afraid he will whip you when you go home?" Long pause.

"No . . . I don't think so," she said. When I asked her, "Does your father's behavior influence your view of God the Father?" all she could do was nod, look downward and cry.

Fourth, *pressure from parents to excel in college often creates conflict over how their children spend time on campus.* Even when parents hold to the same Christian faith, they frequently disapprove of "too much" involvement with parachurch ministries that distracts them from pure academia.

FAMILIES AND LEADERS

It is one thing to become a Christian. That in itself may cause conflict with our parents, especially those of different faiths. To become a Christian leader can jack up the tension between child and parent to a whole new level *even if the parents profess Christian faith.*

In my work with Asian American college students and young adults, I am overwhelmed by the stories of what their discipleship has cost them.

While some have been forsaken by family for simply choosing to follow Jesus (often when leaving the family religion of Hinduism, Buddhism, Shintoism, Islam, etc.), many, *many* more suffer persecution when following him wholeheartedly leads them down paths that shatter their parents' dreams for their lives.

When five Asian American InterVarsity staff were asked to write a discipleship book for young Asian American believers, *Following Jesus Without Dishonoring Your Parents* was the title chosen.[16] How to simultaneously honor one's parents while following Jesus became the consistent and dominant theme that emerged as a central issue in nearly every chapter.

During one of our two writing retreats to work on the book, we were given a living parable of what our book was addressing. David, one of our young Asian American staff, had been beckoned home by his parents. His mom had threatened him: leave staff or I will kill myself. Mom and Dad had sent their oldest son to perhaps the most prestigious university in the country. All their sacrifices had been made for the expected payoff that their son would enter a respectable career and get rich. Becoming an Inter-Varsity staff worker *"who 'begged' others to allow him to work with the cultic club he had given his life to in college"* was not on their top three or thirty list.

In between discussions of various chapters (like "Pressure, Perfectionism and Performance," "Your Parents Love You, My Parents Love Me" and "Honor and Obey ") we called David to see how things were going. We listened, gave bits of advice and prayed for him on the phone. No, his mom didn't kill herself but both parents suffered incredible mental, emotional and physical anguish. And because they were Christians, their faith was challenged to the core.

As we went back to the book, it was clear our book couldn't just give nice principles or address "what if" situations. *Following Jesus Without Dishonoring Your Parents* had to deal with the stuff of life young Asian Americans are often faced with.

For several years after, David lived with the burden of displeasing his parents. At times, it felt unbearable. A year ago, his mom was diagnosed with stage IV stomach cancer. One evening while he was visiting them, his mom called David over to the sofa on which she was resting. Tears streaming down her cheeks, she took hold of David's hand.

"Davey, there's something I've been wanting to say to you for a long time now," she said. "*I'm so sorry. I'm so sorry.* I know I caused you so much pain in the past few years. I should have supported you and just loved you. I'm so sorry, Davey." David and his mom reconciled.

A few days later, David and his wife shared with his mom and dad their desire to serve God overseas, in hopes of receiving their blessing. They were very nervous. David wrote later:

> We were afraid that this would bring about more conflict and that they would feel abandoned by our move. Instead, Dad responded, "It's okay. We think it's okay. You know, we now think that what's most important is that you live a fulfilling life, a happy life. If it will make you happy to go to overseas, then go ahead."

David's father started tearing up. He continued:

> "You know, I've been reflecting so much on my life this past year. I realized that all my dreams have come true. I came to this country, have been given a stable job, two wonderful sons, Mom. I want your dreams to come true."

Then David heard the words he had been praying for and longing to hear for years: "*We support you.*" A few weeks later, David's mom died.[17]

Every three years, we gather all the Asian American staff in InterVarsity Christian Fellowship together for a week of fellowship, teaching and encouragement. At each gathering, we have a time where we invite those to come forward whose decision to serve on InterVarsity staff has brought about family conflicts. Generally, one of every three staff comes forward. We then invite senior staff to pray for each of them. Cries of "They hate what I'm doing with my life!" and "I just want Dad to say he's proud of me—just once!" and "I don't think I can keep doing this without their blessing!" fill the air. The wave of emotion sweeps over the rest of us, nearly knocking us over.

Make no mistake, while there is anger, bitterness and resentment, Asian Americans love their families. That is why it hurts so much when we choose a path different from the one our parents have chosen or desired for us. Martin Luther King Jr. said it well: "There is only great disappointment where there is great love."

LIVING LIMINALLY

Liminality is a fancy word meaning "a place of in-between-ness." No matter how fluent our English is, how hip and American we dress, how easily we seem to hang with non-Asian Americans, we live in a liminal world. Liminality is the fifth strand of our Asian DNA.

We are always in between, with a foot in this world, a foot in that world. As one writer puts it:

> The liminal person is one who has internalized the norms of a particular group but is not completely recognized by the members of that group as being a legitimate member. As long as this relationship prevails, one's role on countless situations will be ill-defined, or defined in different ways by the individual and the group as a whole. Such liminality leads to uncertainty, ambivalence, and the fear of rejection and failure.[18]

Usually it isn't a balanced in-betweenness. One foot leans more heavily than the other. The closer one is to the immigration experience, generally the greater the lean toward their ethnicity. One might feel more comfortable speaking English but still speaks Korean with their parents or with their close Korean friends. Korean is still their "heart language."

Liminality jostles my spiritual development because if I don't have a clear sense of both my Asian and American identities, I don't always know how to best apply scriptural truths. Living in two worlds also takes a lot of psychic energy. When I attend a bilingual service at my Chinese church and thirty minutes later play baseball with my all-white-but-me team, it's usually not until about the third inning before I've "fully arrived."

There's no simple solution to living liminally. Acknowledging it's real and it affects you is a good first step. Knowing which side you favor or lean more heavily on helps self-understanding. Give yourself grace when you do something odd due to living liminally.

Liminality is not all angst producing. It also brings a richness and unpredictability to our lives nonminorities don't get to experience. Life is never boring!

All five of these—Confucianism, shame, suffering, our families and liminality—are built into the warp and woof of our lives. We may not be able to quote Confucius's *Analects*. We may not tell someone, "My *han* level is high today—it would be best if you kept your distance." We may not wear badges that say "I'm suffering today—please hug me," or "I don't do guilt. I do shame." We might not tell someone about some deep family hurts the first time we meet. But if we look beneath our surface, they're there and they affect our spiritual lives as leaders.

3 ARE WE ALL THAT DIFFERENT?

<hr>

I was speaking to the Rutgers University Chinese Christian Fellowship when Janice, a recent graduate, approached me. She said, "When you were introduced, they said you're leading an Asian American leadership workshop tomorrow night at Rutgers Community Christian Church. Do you really think being an Asian American leader is any different than say, being a Caucasian leader?"

The question behind her question, I'm guessing, was, "Is it worth my while to come out for the workshop or should I just stay at home and read Stephen Covey's or John Maxwell's latest book on leadership?"

My three-minute explanation of "Yes!" obviously didn't quite cut it for Janice. She was among the missing the next night, but her question stayed with me.

Are Asian Americans so substantially different that the leadership training for the majority culture doesn't work that well for most Asian Americans?

My musings have brought me back to the same answer time and again: Yes.

YES!

While our addresses, education, dress, careers and the teams we root for may be the same as that of non-Asian Americans, Asian Americans are different at some foundational levels. I have felt the differences the most when I have been in leadership roles. Over the years I have led Asian American, white and multiethnic teams. Each has called for a different leadership style. If we are leading in a multiethnic or primarily white context, to be effective we may need to lead in a way that doesn't feel totally comfortable and natural to us. Conversely, if we have deeply assimilated into Western culture, leading in an Asian American context may be awkward.

The settings I am most comfortable and am most likely to contribute in are with individuals or *small* groups made up of people who are good listeners and internal processors with soft voices. I seem to contribute less in groups where we jump from one topic to another without closure and when the group has several loud extroverts.

When leading or participating in white or multiethnic groups, air space is often at a premium. I need to jump in with both feet and a louder than natural voice or I will lose my chance to influence.

I have watched dynamic and assertive Asian American leaders ratchet down several notches when they're in non-Asian American settings. They appear less confident, don't volunteer their opinions or ideas without prompting, and give way to those more gregarious rather than fight them for air time.

When I was appointed as InterVarsity's area director for Florida, it meant going to meetings with five other area directors and the regional director for the Southeast. That group was composed of an African American man, five white men and me. Our meetings were stimulating and exciting for those who processed ideas quickly, spoke loudly and didn't mind cutting off another person to propose their own solution. I wasn't good at any of those things so I rarely contributed.

Once a teammate took me aside and asked me, "Paul, why don't you share more? I know you have good stuff to offer." My response: "Everyone's fighting for air time. I can't compete."

My experiences in this group helped me see some things about my communication style. Any group larger than four or five feels too large for me to chime in with my ideas without waiting my turn or being called on. I tend to shut down verbally. I usually bounce my ideas off someone during a break before bringing it up with the whole group. If I receive positive strokes it emboldens me to contribute when we're back together. Being asked to contribute also frees me to speak up, while others may feel put on the spot. I appreciate being asked to speak on an area in which I have some expertise. I am very uncomfortable volunteering, "Can I give that talk?"

While I would love whatever group I am in to adjust to what feels comfortable to me, I don't have that luxury. Paul's words to Timothy apply: "For God did not give us a spirit of timidity, but a spirit of power, of love and of self-discipline" (2 Tim 1:7). For me, it takes power, love and self-discipline to come out of my comfort zone in order to make a contribution that will help the group. If I choose to opt out physically or mentally, I will be filled with resentment. I owe it to the group to resist that.

My own discomfort in some groups has helped me lead other groups. When I spot people who don't feel free to share, I try extra hard to include them. When I sense that one member's gregariousness keeps a quieter member from contributing, I'll mention it to the former during a coffee break or after the meeting. Often they are surprised. One, surprised to be told their talkativeness might be excessive. Two, surprised that it can cause someone else to shut down.

My preferred style of decision-making is "Can I get back to you on that tomorrow?" But to do so is to lose the chance to shape the decision that is being made on the spot. Reflection is often not highly valued. But in Asian American groups, silence is more than the absence of words. It is the setting for ideas to coalesce in our minds with carefully chosen words to follow. Silence often signifies respect for the idea being discussed.

In multiethnic settings, it's perfectly normal to volunteer for choice assignments. But in an Asian American gathering, it feels presumptuous, aggressive and even arrogant to raise a hand and say, "I'll do it." When asked to take on a task, our reflexive response is often, "Oh, Joe can do it better. Let Joe do it."

However, when the offer isn't repeated to us, we are offended. "I know I can do a better job than Joe; why didn't they see that and ask me again?" What is called respect in one culture looks like apathy in another. In some Asian cultures, it is impolite to accept until asked at least four times.

When Janice asked me at Rutgers if leading in an Asian American setting is really any different, I asked her, "Have you every told anyone 'Shut up!' in an Asian American context?" Her look of horror said it all.

There have been times in multiethnic settings when I have done just that with coworkers who were also good friends. It was perfectly acceptable. For them, it said, "Paul is comfortable enough with me to communicate on my terms and not just his." That is, after they get over the shock of hearing "Shut up!" come from my lips.

In some African American congregations where there is a lot of give-and-take between preacher and parishioner, a loud "Shut up!" is music to the speaker's ears. It means her incisive point just came through loud and clear. Translation of "Shut up!": The truth of your words pierces my heart. It's not what I want to hear but what I need. In other words, *don't* shut up.

"How long does it take an Asian American group to decide where to have lunch?" was the second question I asked Janice. Her "ha, been there, done that" laugh said it all. We don't pick a restaurant until all voices have been heard and all are at least copacetic with the final choice. A softly whispered "I don't care that much for Italian" instantly kills a trip to the Olive Garden.

Gray hair in campus ministry is usually the kiss of death in Western settings. Translation: out of touch, of another generation, can't relate anymore, reminds me of my parents, try Grecian Formula.

With Asian Americans, it's the exact opposite. Age is revered, gray hair is chic. "How many years have you been on staff?" always comes up in InterVarsity gatherings of Asian American staff. Over twenty years of service usually draws gasps of awe accompanied by bows of "I'm not worthy." And they mean it.

One Asian American parachurch worker told me of his struggles with his new supervisor. "We're about the same age," he said. "What does he have to offer me?" I've had conversations on the same topic with Caucasians: "This is cool! My new boss is not way older than me. We have a lot in common. We swap music CDs. We even hang out together."

As we become part of multiethnic churches and fellowships, we learn new dance steps. That means things will be awkward at first. If a second language is involved, like having Korean as the first language at home and church and English everywhere else, ratchet up the difficulty of going back and forth with ease and grace. But don't stop dancing. The two worlds really are different, and moving in and out of them takes practice and skill.

CHARTING OUR DIFFERENCES

Leadership Education for Asian Pacifics (or LEAP; their term "Asian Pacifics" includes Pacific Islanders) is a secular organization that provides exactly what their name says. They have produced a helpful chart showing some of the differences between Asian and Western or mainstream cultures (see table 3.1).

LEAP's chart is a good example of the impact of Confucianism. Confucius's five virtues of kindness, uprightness, decorum, wisdom and faithfulness along with his emphasis on *lǐ*—a combination of morality and etiquette, custom and ritual—are woven throughout the right column. They're clearly evident in the sections describing self-control/discipline and obedience to authority.

As LEAP is quick to point out, these are generalities and there are always exceptions. What the chart helpfully does is give us some categories to reflect upon. For those of us brought up primarily in mainstream environs, we've learned "left column" behaviors. If we didn't we would never survive. "Right column" behavior feels more natural but doesn't help us fit in when we are in multiethnic or mainstream situations.

Changing behavior, however, is easier said than done. It takes time, practice and causes low-grade schizophrenia. What happens if we choose not to change and adapt when we enter mainstream situations?

LEAP has charted some behaviors often found in Asian Americans and then how they might be interpreted by someone from the mainstream culture (see table 3.2).

My first response to this chart was "Those are just stereotypes! I'm not like that!" After reacting, I worked through the list and could see where these left-column qualities, often thought if not spoken by non-Asian Americans, could indeed elicit the right-column interpretations.

I asked myself, *Which of these qualities do I possess?* "Limited facial expression, demonstrative behavior" brought a quick, "Yup, that's me."

For years, I actually took pride in having a stoic demeanor and being

Table 3.1. Asian American vs. Mainstream Values

Mainstream (Western) Values	**Asian American Values**
Spontaneity/casualness ■ importance of social skills, informal relationships, small talk ■ all right to show all kinds of emotion ■ promote flexibility	Self control/discipline ■ speaks only when spoken to ■ inner stamina/strength to tolerate crisis ■ solid performer ■ doesn't show emotions
Respect for change/control over one's environment/belief in self-determination ■ more risk-taking ■ more aggressive ■ concrete/strive for explicitness ■ initiates	Fatalism ■ acceptance of ambiguity and uncertainty ■ more patient, more ready to accept things as they are
All right to question authority ■ anticipates problem areas, opportunities and initiates appropriate actions	Obedient to authority ■ respect those who lead ■ loyal ■ trustworthy ■ follow through on assignments
Cites accomplishments ■ visibility (individual) is all right ■ rewards individual for outstanding actions ■ power is perceived as individual power	Humbleness ■ low individual visibility ■ power is shared with others
Tough, individualistic and authoritative leadership ■ individual leadership ■ individual responsibility ■ independence ■ "pioneer spirit"	Collective decision-making ■ proving the sources ■ collective responsibility and ownership ■ interdependence ■ strong teamwork

These are generalizations and may not totally reflect the values of specific Asian Pacific Americans (APAs) or specific APA groups (excerpts from Jo S. Uehara). As we review these values and corresponding actions, it becomes clear that an organization rewards those who hold the dominant cultural values at the managerial level. Values of both groups are important and valuable. Many of those who have lived several generations in the United States may find themselves holding values from both cultures.

hard to read. I thought, *It sure worked for Bruce Lee.* But when I realized
most of my social interactions didn't call for martial arts expertise, I saw
how "blank face" could come across as "has no investment in the matter
at hand, no feeling; therefore seems to have no vulnerability, which could
be a threat."

When I was really truthful with myself, I knew that I liked the power
it gave me over those who preferred conversations in their relationships.
Since then, I've worked at being more expressive and volunteering feelings even when it didn't feel quite natural.

One time "limited facial expression" did get me out of a bind. Several
years ago, I was taking a late evening ride on MARTA, Atlanta's rapid transit, to the airport. I was loaded down with luggage and my laptop. After a
few stops, I noticed I was the only one in my car, along with four young
guys in their late teens or early twenties. I overheard one say, "Should we
take him?" Another responded, "Do you think he knows kung fu?" I pre-
tended to study some notes but I knew a response of some sort on my part
was soon to be requested.

The night before while channel surfing, I happened upon a Jean-
Claude Van Damme martial arts flick. Margaret, who thinks *A Room with
a View* is exciting, walked by. She asked with obvious disapproval, "Why
are you watching *that*?" Since I had no good answer, I just gave that solid
male grunt that can mean almost anything.

Back on MARTA. One of the four guys got my attention, saying, "Hey,
man, do you know kung fu?" I looked up at them and gave them ten sec-
onds of my best Van Damme blank stare impersonation. Then I broke into
his little crooked smile. At that my four new friends backed off, then
jumped out at the next stop—without my luggage and laptop.

Friends, don't necessarily try this on your rapid transit.

BIBLICAL ENCOURAGEMENT

Our Bible helps us not to lose hope as we can often feel like strangers in
a strange land. The Old Testament is a survival epic of aliens holding on
to the things of value in one's culture and adapting when necessary.

Moses and Esther (covered later in chapter seven) in particular have

Table 3.2. **Possible Misinterpretations of Asian American Behavior.** Adapted from LEAP's Leadership Management Institute curriculum, 1997.

Asian American Behavior		Possible Interpretation by a Person from Mainstream Culture
▪ quiet, doesn't speak up	→	▪ isn't interested, doesn't understand or knows it all
▪ not assertive (according to the dominant value)	→	▪ lacks leadership, could not be authoritative when necessary
▪ limited facial expression, demonstrative behavior	→	▪ has no investment in the matter at hand, no feeling; therefore seems to have no vulnerability, which could be a threat
▪ avoids making presentations, speaking in public	→	▪ not interested, lacks knowledge or information, unwilling to share, secretive, lacks confidence
▪ indirect eye contact	→	▪ lacks respect, shows no interest, no confidence, is unable to read nonverbal cues of those he or she is talking to
▪ doesn't complain, good worker	→	▪ is exploitable
▪ doesn't socialize after work	→	▪ is above making friends, unwilling to get to know coworkers or vice-versa, can't be trusted, inscrutable
▪ unwilling to take chances	→	▪ lacks leadership skills to manage a group
▪ speaks with an accent	→	▪ is not credible; doesn't know much; can't speak, read, write or understand English
▪ physically short, small	→	▪ lacks maturity, has limited ability to influence, organize, motivate others

been soulmates for me. Abraham, Joseph, Daniel and his friends, Naomi and Ruth have also gotten me through times of aloneness. My heart reverberates with the psalmist writing in exile:

> By the rivers of Babylon we sat and wept
> when we remembered Zion.
> How can we sing the songs of the LORD
> while in a foreign land? (Ps 137:1, 4)

How many immigrant Asian Americans have felt the same from time to time?

The New Testament is also a crosscultural guide. People who feel like the minority are everywhere. Jews who have embraced the Messiah now must navigate carefully amongst their own, especially relatives. These same believers are now being asked to welcome those once viewed as dogs—Gentiles—into their family of faith. Those sent out as the first missionaries venture onto totally foreign turf. Leadership teams are now comprised of Jews and a wide array of Gentiles and from different vocations and socioeconomic standings.

When we as Asian Americans interact within the mainstream culture, we don't enter alone. Scripture gives us much to identify with and provides us with hope and encouragement.

Even more helpful is knowing that behind our Bible is our God who walked with many a lonely and confused alien and helped them sing in a land that felt so foreign and unaccepting. We don't go alone. Immanuel—God with us—walks and sings.

4

BECOMING A PRETTY GOOD LEADER I

Who They Are

Leading is tough. Each situation brings its own complexity, and each leader faces unique challenges because of background, temperament and more.

For me, being a leader who is also Asian American brings some particular difficulties. For example, we value being a member in good standing of our community. We'll do practically anything not to rock the boat. Being a leader corrupts our "one for all and all for one" mindset. It sets me apart from those with whom I want to blend in. Critiquing someone feels too much like criticizing them. I don't want to be singled out as a failure or not pulling my weight and letting others down so I certainly don't want to point the finger at others. It feels like I'm betraying them.

I guess it comes down to this: I don't want to be the nail that sticks out. Leaders simply stick out.

Being a leader in Asian American settings has complexities as well. After several decades of leading in non-Asian American settings, it was initially a breath of fresh air to lead Asian Americans. Overall folks were quiet, childlike and fun-loving, always showing appreciation and respectful of me as an elder, and we had great snacks at meetings. The list could go on.

The honeymoon ended after the first few years. I began to see the negative flipside of the qualities that first enamored me. At times I hate how we can't speak truthfully with each other because we want to save face for the other person. At times I hate how important family is and how every major decision has to clear the mom and dad screen. At times I hate how

WHEN LEADING REEKS

I hate that the buck stops with me.

I hate the loneliness at the top.

I hate knowing I'm being talked about without me there to defend myself.

I hate it when I step out on a limb . . . and then I turn around to see someone sawing it off.

I hate it most when I've invested years in that limb-cutter. I really hate that.

I hate it when I do something good, really good, but know it's not godly to let people know it was me who actually did it, so it leaves me feeling underappreciated.

I hate doing performance appraisals for people floundering with their job. I especially hate getting that "Why don't you just shoot me?" look when I tell them they should think about another position or role.

I hate losing my friendships with my peers because I'm now overseeing them and we're no longer equals.

I hate missing my favorite TV program because our leadership team chose that night to meet and I couldn't quite tell them why it wasn't the best time for me.

I hate how leadership in Christendom pays so poorly and to ask for a raise is considered unspiritual.

much longer it takes to get things done because everyone's voice counts and we have to have consensus before we move. At times I hate how hypersensitive Asians Americans are and how I have to always check to see if their feelings were hurt over something I said or didn't say. At times I hate how women are treated poorly, how we can't live without their behind-the-scenes work, but we forbid them to lead. At times I hate how we esteem white people so highly it's almost impossible to have a true peer friendship with any of them. At times I hate how parents keep comparing their children.

Do I sound a little upset, a bit angry? You got that right. But for the most part, the anger isn't too deep and it doesn't linger too long. Sharing space with my frustrations is the boatload of blessings of leadership.

Why do I lead when the "hate" list is longer than the "love" list? Mainly because being a leader allows me the remarkable privilege of influencing lives. I am willing to put up with a lot of stuff if I can influence others.

I have led Christians and I have led non-believers. I've led all-Asian American groups, multiethnic groups and white groups. Occasionally I've led African American groups. I've managed, coordinated or co-led youth baseball teams, evangelism projects, a book-writing team, small group Bible studies, a church basketball team, training conferences, birthday parties, grape and lettuce boycotts on behalf of Mexican American farmworkers, a pastor's performance appraisal task force, a college newspaper staff, a blood drive, Sunday School classes, a Japanese American Citizens League chapter, I-Dabble-at-Scrabble and I-Ogle-at-Boggle tournaments, a countywide public service fair, readers' theater groups, crosscultural training, a pastor search committee, programs to welcome new leaders and programs to honor departing employees.

> ## WHEN LEADING ROCKS
> *Being a leader means I've been given opportunity to shape events.*
>
> *Being a leader means I can initiate change rather than wait for change to happen through someone else.*
>
> *Being a leader means I no longer have to be a victim. I can change things.*
>
> *Being a leader means I can shape my days, weeks and months and take vacations when I choose.*
>
> *Being a leader means I often get to pick the people I lead.*
>
> *Being a leader means seeing someone's life changed by God before my very eyes. It just doesn't get a whole lot better than when that happens.*

I started leading before I knew better and have been leading ever since. Over thirty-five years of being a leader has organized and shaped my life. I first led out of need. I still lead out of need. It's not the headaches and the pain I need, though sometimes I wonder. It's mostly the need to influence and the desire to be helpful. It's a way I can serve people well. As a follower of Jesus, it's the best way I know how to be a productive member of his kingdom.

There are times I lead really well and feel like it's what I've been created for. I do the Tiger Woods fist pump almost better than Tiger himself (when alone, of course). Then there are times when my leadership stinks up the joint and I want to slink away quietly and figure out what went wrong.

GAMBLING FOR JESUS

One of those times was spring quarter, sophomore year.

I had just been chosen president of the InterVarsity fellowship at Cal Poly-San Luis Obispo. The new leadership team began meeting to get ready for the next year. Our expectations for what God might do through us were soaring. I was the only holdover from the previous year's leadership team, so I was looked to for seasoned experience. I was also the only Asian American on the team and one of two in the entire fellowship.

My first move was to rename the group. Cal Poly Christian Fellowship sounded too normal. The Jesus movement was in full bloom. One Way bumper stickers were everywhere. I decided we'd call ourselves "One Way Fellowship"!

We waited a few weeks to unveil it to the fellowship but we would greet each other with our secret greeting of "Owf," as in One Way Fellowship. As in "barf" without the "b" and "r." Honestly, we did this. When one of our new leaders wisely asked, "How will that make the other Christian organizations on campus feel?" we came to our senses and canned that fabulous new name.

We were just warming up.

Campus Crusade for Christ was holding a "meninar" (similar to their "feminar" for female students). Feeling ecumenical, I signed up. Part of our training on being a godly male was to go out on a date and then meet at midnight at a local coffee shop with the other men and discuss our dates. Seriously.

I was always looking for an excuse for a date, so this training program was no problem. Discussing how my date went seemed a bit odd, but I figured Campus Crusade didn't get to be so large by making lame moves. I trusted them.

I asked out Ally, a member of the new leadership team. We had a nice dinner. I even paid. Walking across the parking lot to my car, I spotted a carnival set up in a far corner of the lot. Why not? The night was young, I wasn't due at the coffee shop for two hours, and frankly, I loved those parking lot carnivals.

We went on several rides. I was still paying. Growing up, I always loved the games of chance at the summer Obon bazaar our local Buddhist church held. Ring toss, dime toss, goldfish toss, stuffed animal toss—they all plugged me into my Buddhist heritage. When I saw the game area, it was a no-brainer.

Ally and I ended up at a game where you throw little balls down a chute. They bounce around then land on numbers. Either a really low total number or a really high total number would win big money.

As the game master explained, *really big money.*

Our leadership team had just planned our outreaches for the following year. We had come up with big plans that would take big money, *really big money.*

With each round we played, the game master would tell us we came *so close* to winning. In fact, so close, he would let our "so close" scores accumulate, giving us a shot at *really, really big money.*

Ally and I looked at each other. Our looks said it all: *Can you believe it? God is going to answer our prayers by providing our fellowship's budget right here, right now, when we win this silly little game!*

About $75 later, we had come so close but no cigar, as the game master put it. But because we were a cute couple and he was starting to really like us, he said, "Tell you what I'll do. If you come back first thing tomorrow morning when we open and before the crowds come, I will let you pick up right where you left off. You are so close, you're sure to win!"

"Really? You would do that for us? See you at ten tomorrow!"

I went on to meet the Crusade men at the coffee shop while Ally called each member of our leadership team, all six of them, to ask them to pray. I reported in on dinner and the Ferris wheel but somehow forgot to mention the game. Asian American face-saving was working well that night.

The next morning, all but Susan agreed to accompany us and be our praying team. The newest believer on our leadership team, she refused to come, objecting, "You guys! That's gambling! God's not going to honor gambling!"

We excused her lack of spiritual sophistication to her newness to the faith. The others of us piled into Dave's pickup. When we got to the parking lot we asked God to give us the *big money.* We were convinced he would come through for us and deliver the year's budget. This was too easy.

An hour later, we quietly walked away . . . without the big money. In fact, Ally and I walked away a total $135 poorer (that would be $562 in 2003 dollars!). This time I didn't totally treat; she coughed up $50 of her own money. The other leadership team members were equally chagrined at our being taken by a carnival rube. We didn't discuss the carnival in future leadership meetings. It was our little secret.

A few weeks later, we were off to leadership camp. For a week, we gathered to receive leadership training and be with leaders from other fellowships on the West Coast. We spent hours together as a leadership team to pray, plan and grow together.

One evening as we met, I exploded at the others. "We need to be totally honest with each other! When I blow it with you, I want to know! I–"

"Paul, you're blowing it, right now," said Doug, our staff worker.

After the smoke had cleared and the meeting ended, he took me aside. "Paul, I want you to think about stepping down as the president. I'd like you to switch places with Dave. He becomes the president and you become the literature coordinator."

I was stunned by Doug's words. I had failed as president. The school year hadn't even started and I was getting the hook. How was I going to face the fellowship when we returned in the fall? Literature coordinator? I hardly read my own textbooks.

I went straight to bed. The next morning when the breakfast bell rang, I couldn't get out of bed. When I tried to lift myself up, my arms gave way. I was literally sick from Doug's suggestion. I stayed in bed until that afternoon, which gave me a lot of time to reflect and pray. This was good because I was too ashamed to face my fellow leaders.

I couldn't miss all three meals so I dragged myself to dinner and found Doug. "I believe God wants me to be president," I said.

Doug responded too casually given the bad day I had endured: "That's fine, Paul. I was just making a suggestion. Stay president."

Gambling away all my money (and Ally's) and leading so erratically at camp ended up being turning points for me as a leader. In the past, the shame of doing stupid things would have buried me. Instead, in the context of forgiving ministry partners, I could keep leading and developing. Grace happened.

The next two years of campus leadership were a greenhouse for my formation as a leader. With fellow learning-leaders who encouraged, affirmed and challenged me, I was on the road to becoming *a pretty good leader.*

QUALITIES OF A PRETTY GOOD LEADER

These days my second office is a Panera Bread Company in Atlanta. My "cubicle" is the booth on the left in the far back of this terrific bagel and coffee place, fifteen feet from the men's room. With unlimited refills and pretty good jazz and classical music playing through the PA, it's a great place to ruminate. Last summer, I took several weeks to reflect on leadership and Asian American leadership in particular.

Much of my initial musings revolved around two questions: *What is a leader responsible for?* and *What do I think is most important in developing as a pretty good leader?* I reflected on, not so much about what the leadership gurus said, though I respect their work, but more on how I was led, how I led others and what excellent leaders around me did so well.

Why a "pretty good leader" and not a "great" or "excellent" leader?

I play in a men's senior baseball league for geezers over thirty-eight. I've been on the Atlanta Astros for eight seasons. Our best power hitter is Randy Hansen. Often, when he's at the plate, his good friend and teammate Kenny Roberts will shout encouragement from the dugout, "Pretty good hitter up there, Randy Hansen, pretty good hitter."

Clearly Randy is more than a "pretty good" hitter. But to hear, "Knock it over the fence, big guy" doesn't help, it just creates who-needs-it pressure. All of us who do any sort of leading don't want to be just pretty good, we want to be great. But it doesn't help to operate with that kind of pressure from those on our team. Just being a leader creates enough internal pressure in itself. We're our own worst critics. We need others to bring perspective about our leadership.

Here are the qualities I came up with, followed by prayers of my heart.

A pretty good leader is someone who

- is being tutored or mentored or discipled by a person who is accessible, soft-hearted, growing, teachable and in touch with reality, and who has suffered or understands suffering

  Lord, I can't and won't lead all by my lonesome. You need to give me some-one who is at least a few steps ahead of me in the faith and as a leader. I need an authentic, real leader who has walked a road similar to the one I'm now on, someone who won't self-edit his advice but will give it to me straight. I need someone who's not afraid to lose our friendship by telling me the truth about myself.

- has dealt with or is dealing with significant past events or relationships and is willing to get professional help if needed

  I have been in counseling for several years to get help for several issues that were destroying me and those I most love. Lord, you know how much I hate counseling, how I hate having to reveal my junk to someone. Most of all, I hate counseling because each time I walk through that door I am admitting I can't take care of my life by myself.

  Stuffing it down is much easier but it is a slow death for me and others. I refuse to kill more people by living in denial. Lord, give me courage to face those things in the dark corners of my heart that scare me to death when I think about bringing them to the light of day.

- admits mistakes, asks forgiveness from those they have injured by their mistakes, including those whom they exercise authority over

  I wish my bad decisions only hurt myself, but they often impact those whom I care dearly about. Help me never to be an inerrant leader who is above both messing up and picking up the pieces of the mess with the injured par-ty. Help me to see quickly when I have hurt someone by my actions, then give me the courage to just as quickly apologize so they don't start accusing themselves for "my bad."

  Lord Jesus, forgive me for how my mistakes have hurt V, D, F, P, G, M, S, H, M, D, K, P, E and S among others, some that I am probably totally clue-less about.

- is comfortable leading and being led by person of the other gender

I confess that leading would be simpler and more cut and dried if my bosses and those I supervised were all men, especially if they all liked sports and action movies. But you know that I need women in my life or I will become two-dimensional and more closed-minded. It's usually been women who have helped me see my blind spots and cared enough about me to point them out, even risking my anger or cold shoulder. Help me to overcome my demons, fears and prejudices so I will invite these women into my life.

- has interests outside of their major realm of responsibility that provide rest, diversion, recharging and perspective

Lord, when I give my whole life to ministry, I become a dangerous person. I lose perspective. I forget the real world out there. I begin thinking that what I do is more important than it really is. Help me to always have outlets—like playing baseball—that keep my world broad and force me to get close to people I might normally disdain. When I have those outlets, I know I am more effective in ministry. Hitting a double can keep a smile on my face for a long time.

As I work with young Asian American leaders—generally those between twenty and their mid-thirties—I'm mostly encouraged about what I see in relation to the qualities above.

In many, I see a very teachable spirit and a desire to be mentored and developed. Dealing with past issues and seeking professional help if needed doesn't come naturally, but some are willing to expand their comfort zone if they are convinced this will bring wholeness and health into their lives. Going to a therapist or counselor is countercultural for most Asian Americans, especially those in the first and second generation who have pulled themselves up by their bootstraps. We think, *I should be able to make it on my own. My parents did.*

Admitting mistakes isn't particularly difficult. We do this well, some of us too well. We are quick to own up to our deficiencies and sometimes apologize even when it's not our mistake or faux pas. Peace and harmony can become so high a value we are willing to short-circuit confession and repentance for others.

I see Asian Americans making strides in their willingness to be led by women, even as church and fellowship leadership structures operate subconsciously on Confucian male-dominant hierarchy with women frequently boxed out.

Asian American church leaders often have few outside interests beyond their work and church. It's not unusual to have three or four nights a week taken up with church work. Ministry can become idolatry. When churches permit only men to lead and teach, half of the potential leadership pool is unavailable, causing men to work twice as hard as necessary.

THE LEADERSHIP GIFT

Jeff and I were discussing leadership within his organization. He had been a national leader for decades and leaked with wisdom and a clarity of vision that was at times scary because he rarely missed the mark. One of Jeff's passing comments keeps coming back to me months later: "He's a great person but he doesn't have the gift of leadership."

Said person was recognized as a sage within and outside of the organization of which he and Jeff were a part. He was thoughtful, well-read, a genuine intellectual and frequently asked to be on important task forces. As a leader, his track record didn't match up. He didn't lead well.

Jeff added the logical follow-up conclusion, but one hardly ever acted upon: "We do him a disservice by letting him lead." We assume anyone that bright can lead well. When we discover they can't, awkwardness sets in. How do we dare move such a person out of a leadership role? How can we reassign them to a place where their best gifts are utilized well in a way that doesn't appear to be a demotion?

Months later, in another conversation with Jeff, he told me that it finally happened. The job transfer took place—not without agonizing—and the new position fits much better. The person is experiencing renewed enthusiasm and joy. Jeff's only regret was it should have happened ten years earlier.

The apostle Paul writes, "Just as each of us has one body with many members, and these members do not all have the same function, so in Christ we who are many form one body, and each member belongs to all the others. We have different gifts, according to the grace given us . . . if it is leadership, let him govern diligently" (Rom 12:4-6, 8).

The word *leader* never appears in the New Testament (though it shows up seventy-eight times in the Old Testament). *Leadership* appears but twice, in Romans above and in Acts 1:20. That's it. For all the attention in Christian circles today on leadership development, it is remarkably underemphasized in the New Testament.

Nonetheless, its appearance in Romans 12 is significant. As Paul addresses how the body of Christ is to function well, leadership is one of a handful of gifts needed. When he writes the church in Corinth, he uses a similar word—administration. In this more detailed description of body life found in 1 Corinthians 12:1-31, we're told several things about gifts:

- They're given for our common good.
- The giver and distributor of the gifts is none other than God himself; that makes gifting supernatural.
- There are many gifts, each having a particular and needed role to play.
- All gifts are indispensable; no one gift is better or more needed than another.
- Body parts are interconnected; when one malfunctions, it affects the functioning of other parts.

How does one determine if they have the gifting of leadership spoken of in these two passages? Slowly and in the context of the body of Christ.

Because the gifts are for the fortifying of the body, we should pay attention to the impact our actions have on our communities. What do those in the community say about the ways I am involved? How are they blessed by me? In what ways have they experienced growth in their faith because of my impact on them?

First, let the body of which you are an active part help determine your gifting. Second, be patient as you try to figure out what gifts God has given you.

It wasn't until my thirties that I could distinguish what my gifting was. I had hunches along the way, but when asked what my gifts were, my usual response was, "Uh . . . what do *you* think my gifts are?" (When in doubt, always answer a question with another question!)

I may have been particularly dense in not being able to answer that question definitively at an earlier stage of my life. I can't tell you how many Sunday school classes I attended and books I read on the topic of spiritual gifts. I took those little tests, filled out charts and still wasn't sure. I made sure being personally stumped didn't hamper ministering to others. My overriding life theme was to serve others effectively.

While serving in my twenties and early thirties, the fog dissipated. In the end, from the first-century lists in 1 Corinthians and Romans—which are illustrative of gifts that are good for the body (and are not exhaustive)—I identified leadership as my primary gifting. I prayed for tongues, thought miraculous powers would be cool and hoped serving wasn't my gifting. For this season it seems leadership is what I have to offer others.

How did I figure that out? Primarily by the affirmation of those whom I led in various settings. Sure I made mistakes, some of the truly bonehead variety, but *God used my leadership to bless others and often to accomplish what we set out to do.* I knew that because they made a point to tell me.

If you're in college or in your early twenties, my advice is to not lose much sleep figuring out your gifting. Rather, serve the body of Christ wholeheartedly and give yourself with abandon to help it become healthy and vibrant. If you're asked to clean a bathroom, do it. If you are asked to speak or teach, do it. You might be asked to do both; do them both. They are both streams from the same source: servanthood. As you serve, your gifts will emerge, much like a diamond from coal. In time, you'll know.

Paul was so right when he ends his most extensive gifts treatise: "And now I will show you the most excellent way" (1 Cor 12:31).

Love. Oh, yeah.

5

Becoming a Pretty Good Leader II

What They Choose to Do

J ust do it.

That line comes from Nike, not the Bible, but it's good advice when it comes to developing as a leader. A pretty good leader doesn't become one, as we might say in the South, by "a'sittin' and a'chewin'."

A pretty good—what I really mean is very good—leader is intentional in several areas. These are the ways leaders live out love—that "most excellent way."

LEADERS WORK WITH PEOPLE THEY DON'T NATURALLY CHOOSE TO BE WITH

I don't like people who talk loud, don't listen to others, smell like they need a bath, have a physical infirmity, aren't high achievers, wear eyelid rings, drive slow in the fast lane, drive fast in the slow lane, are overweight and have double and triple chins, pass gas in public, have coffee breath, send e-mails with typographical errors, try to slip into the express lane with more than fifteen items, mumble, ask me to repeat myself when I mumble, are always late to meetings, think professional wrestling is a sport.

In other words, I don't like people who are like me on my bad days. In my perfect parallel universe, I wouldn't be guilty of any of the above. What I don't like in others is usually what I despise when it shows up in my own life.

By working with those whom I don't usually choose to be with, I learn to accept my own irritating shortcomings as well. But because I despise these things in myself and others, I must *choose* to be with people who regularly partake in one or more of the things on my "don't like" list. It won't happen on its own.

When I do, I become a better person. Forgiving others reminds me to forgive myself for the same shortcoming. When I forgive myself, I become less of a perfectionist and less of a pain to be around.

In college, Jim and Nate were two of these people for me. Jim was a committed member of our fellowship. Whenever we gathered, he was there. One annoying quality about Jim was he stuttered. A lot. Sometimes, it seemed like an eternity for Jim to spit it out. He could drive me up a wall; speaking well and clearly is a high value for me.

I noticed that when Jim would slow down, his words would come out more freely. I talked to him about this. He told me that often he would get so excited about expressing himself he didn't realize how badly he was stuttering.

"Jim, can I help?" I asked.

We came up with a plan. I told him when we are in a meeting or gathering and he stuttered, I would touch my nose with my finger. That would signal him to slow down and relax.

Nate was an agriculture major. Taking English was not his reason for being at Cal Poly but it was required for graduation. Writing essays were like roping calves without a decent lasso for him. Being a journalism major, I loved words.

"Nate, I'd be happy to work with you on your essays," I offered.

And did we ever work. Nate's writing skills were easily five or six years below college quality, but he was willing to work hard. Sometimes, we met two to three times over one essay. We watched his low Ds become high Ds. When he got his first C on an essay, I thought the rodeo had come to town, he was so ecstatic. When his grade for the term arrived, we almost had a private party: C-! Yeah, baby!

While I helped Jim and Nate, I was helped even more by growing in patience and acceptance of people not on my "A list."

For many Asian Americans, their Jims and Nates—those with whom they wouldn't naturally spend time—are those of certain nationalities not their own. We can discriminate and be prejudicial with the best of them. One only needs to point out the neighborhoods we live in, the schools we send our children to and the friends we have into our homes to render us guilty as charged. We don't limit our prejudice to non-Asians. Most of us have a particular Asian nationality or several we don't feel fully comfortable calling "family."

LEADERS TAKE CALCULATED RISKS

A leader always has one eye to the future, hoping to discern what move to make a week, a month and three years from today. Good leaders are never satisfied with the "same ol', same ol'." They live for breakthroughs and first place finishes. They are the ones Robert Kennedy pictured when he said, "Some men see things as they are and say, 'Why?' I dream things that never were and say, 'Why not?' "

They are risk-takers but of a certain ilk. Good leaders don't risk with blind faith. The stakes are too high to risk for risk's sake alone—especially when it involves the lives of people entrusted to our care. Our risk-taking must include a reasonable chance of success. General George Patton said it well: "Take calculated risks. That is quite different from being rash."

Another general, Douglas MacAurthur, embodied the "calculating risk-taker" when he boldly led the retaking of the Philippines from the Japanese during World War II and later when he drove North Korea out of South Korea with a daring amphibious landing of Inchon.

In 1933, America was deep in the throes of the Great Depression. The economy was in shambles and citizens were demoralized. More than sixteen million people were unemployed. Many had been out of work for a year or even longer.

As newly elected president Franklin Roosevelt approached the dais for his first inaugural address, he knew he had to bring hope to the embattled citizenry. With the nation gathered around family radios, Roosevelt pledged to "make war" upon the depression. His ringing phrase "We have nothing to fear but fear itself" connected heart-to-heart. He exuded confidence, both in himself as a leader and in the American people. His liking for people came through to them over the radio and in the press.

Even though he made few specific promises in his speech, Americans felt more comfortable under the leadership of a man pledged to experiment than they had under previous President Herbert Hoover's leadership, which had seemed inflexible.[1]

Calculated risk-taking also has personal payoffs. Ever see the looks on the faces of risk-takers on survival shows who scale cliffs, jump out of planes and eat live crickets? They live for the risk.

In business, Truett Cathy, the founder of Chick-fil-A, introduced the unthinkable: close shop on Sundays. A Christian and a family man, Cathy wanted to honor the sabbath and make sure his employees could be with their families at least one day a week. Critics scoffed. He would lose far too much income to be viable.

He writes in *It's Easier to Succeed Than to Fail*, "Our bodies and our minds need time off to recharge. I've accepted that as a principle and honored God by doing it. God has honored us and the business because of it."[2] Cathy's "calculated risk" resulted in creating one of the finest fast food businesses.

LEADERS WORK TOWARD HAVING HEALTHY
FAMILY RELATIONSHIPS

Confucius was right; healthy families lead to a healthy society. Healthy nuclear families are foundational to a thriving Christian community. Broken, fractured or conflicted family relationships impact relationships in the body of Christ.

When Scripture addresses the qualifications for leaders in Christian communities, family relationships are always addressed:

An elder must be blameless, the husband of but one wife, a man whose children believe and are not open to the charge of being wild and disobedient. (Tit 1:6)

If anyone sets his heart on being an overseer, he desires a noble task. He must manage his own family well and see that his children obey him with proper respect. If anyone does not know how to manage his own family, how can he take care of God's church? (1 Tim 3:1, 4-5)

Being a godly husband or wife, mother or father, son or daughter is much harder than being a good leader. I get disgusted with myself when I go through seasons where there is tension in my marriage and I'm speaking at a conference; I'm tempted to act like I have it all together and everything is fine.

What I want to do is interrupt myself, pull myself off of my speaking notes and blurt out, "Hey, there are unresolved issues for me at home. I shouldn't be giving this talk on family relationships. I should be home working things out." But I go back to my notes, grit my teeth and get through it and wait until I get home to work things out.

On the flip side, when life is good at home, I go to those conferences with a skip in my step and a genuine smile.

Asian Americans with siblings should have a jump start in helping others succeed. They instinctively know how to look out for younger siblings. They serve as pathfinders, breaking ground to make it a bit easier for them. When asked to disciple or mentor a newer believer in their church or fellowship, they have the experience and some of the know-how to take them under their wing.

LEADERS TAKE ADVANTAGE OF TRAINING OPPORTUNITIES

Good leaders never stop learning. They're always looking for ways to improve. Terry Morrison, a wise and seasoned campus minister, says it well: "Slow down. Do less. Do better."

There is no shortage of quality workshops and books on leadership development. They cover the waterfront of becoming a better leader, from finding a personal mentor to developing personal mission statements to building character to developing group leading skills to envisioning for the future. They are plentiful in both secular and Christian circles. Ask peers and leaders you admire what resources they would suggest for you.

While there are always trendy, hot leadership approaches that may be quite valid and helpful, the bread and butter areas of leadership development remain constant:

- personal character

- leadership skills (group leading, delegation, envisioning, strategic planning, public speaking, event planning and execution, fiscal responsibility, conflict resolution, problem solving)
- leadership styles

Most books on these topics are not written by Asian Americans or by those who have thought about leadership through our cultural lens. Try reading with these cultural filters on: Is there an appreciation for how my family's values impact my values? Does the author respect a variety of leadership styles or is one "best" style favored (such as vocal vs. soft-spoken and reflective, direct vs. indirect when criticizing things, spoken vs. written communication)? If I adopt the author's values or style will I betray my essence as a unique person?

LEADERS SOCIALIZE WITH NONBELIEVERS

I love Christians most of the time. Fellow believers can encourage, exhort and tell me the truth about myself and about God. I need them.

I will also experience spiritual asphyxiation if all my discretionary time is in Bible studies, church services, prayer meetings, worship experiences, lunch with Christian friends, ad nauseum.

I am most alive when I am spending time with both Christians and non-Christians. I need believers because they are able to speak biblical truth and reality into my life that a nonbeliever simply cannot. I need nonbelievers because they provide me with reality checks.

Several years ago, Mom and I were having one of our heart-to-heart talks. I confessed to her that I was struggling with staying humble. She responded with a look of puzzlement, then said, "What have you accomplished that makes you struggle with being humble?" Zing!

The more leadership responsibilities one takes on in church or fellowship, the more difficult it is to find time to be with those outside the family of faith. There is something inherently imbalanced about the way most churches approach those spiritually mature and gifted in leadership. Do something well? We give you more to do in the church.

And evangelism? We acknowledge it is important, even vital to the life of the church but we leave little space for leaders to have authentic, time-consuming relationships with nonbelievers. Something's really wrong here.

Peter was an elder in my church and a good friend. He was a physician with his own practice. As an elder, Peter taught Sunday school and chaired various committees. His meetings were what you would expect from a harried doctor. A Whopper in one hand, meeting notes in the other, Peter would arrive late, apologize and then lead us with disorganized gusto.

I'd leave those meetings shaking my head. *This is not what Peter is good at. What he's really good at is evangelism. I wish Peter could step down out of formal church leadership and be freed to share his faith.*

When Peter and I would chat, he would mention a spiritually oriented conversation with a patient or a coworker. He would light up. Finally, I told him, "Peter, this is what you are really good at—being with nonbelievers. Sharing your life and your faith with them. I wish you would invest yourself in evangelism instead of being an elder." It never happened, at least during our ten years in that church.

LEADERS ASK FOR FEEDBACK AND INPUT

In my twenties I pictured myself as a leader in his forties and fifties. I would give advice without second-guessing myself, give talks without notes because I knew my subject matter cold, rally the troops with the bravado of a Colin Powell or at least a Phil Jackson. Of course, there was the corner office on the twentieth floor with a fabulous view of the cityscape. That went without saying. Leadership at fifty would be like breathing, second nature.

Oh well.

Some insecurities die far too slowly. Some may never die. I may never feel good about a talk I give unless my wife or a close friend tells me it went well. Silence from those whose opinions mean a lot (probably way too much) to me still shakes me up. From some important people in my life, I need to know I did okay.

In all arenas of leadership—speaking, leading, advising—we must continue to develop. One way we do that is to receive input from others.

In 1973, I had just joined the staff of InterVarsity, fresh out of college. That fall, I was staffing a conference for students in northern Indiana. The topic was evangelism, the speaker was Robert Coleman, author of *The Master Plan of Evangelism* and *One Divine Moment,* which chronicled the Asbury College revival of the 1960s. Both books had a shaping influence on me during college. I was thrilled to be able to hear him speak.

After his first two talks, I was in a quandary. *The man writes so much better than he speaks,* I thought. As a recent graduate, it was so clear to me that he was on a different wavelength than the undergraduates he was addressing. I hated seeing the students go through the rest of the conference as frustrated as I was. Clearly, I had no choice. After lunch on Saturday, I sought him out and we found a table in the emptying cafeteria.

I looked over to the next table where Al, one of my coworkers, was finishing a cup of coffee. His back was to me but he was close enough to hear our conversation. I hoped he would be praying for Dr. Coleman to "get it" and either make wholesale changes to his remaining two talks or graciously give the speaking slots to some younger staff (guess who?) who could "connect."

After a few pleasantries, I jumped in with both feet. "Dr. Coleman, I really like your books. I don't know how to say this, but you just aren't connecting with the students here. Your approach may work at the seminary you teach at but these college students are at a different place. You're just not getting through to them."

I must have missed seeing Al's head snap back as he listened in. Dr. Coleman responded, "Paul, thank you so much for bringing this to my attention. What can I do to improve my last two talks?" Of course, I proceeded to give him my suggestions. He asked me to elaborate on some of them. He then thanked me and said he needed to go back to his room to rework the talks.

I felt good. Perhaps God had used me, a new first-year twenty-two-year-old staff worker to salvage the conference. I couldn't wait to hear the talks and see how my advice made them stronger.

Al came up and jolted me out of my self-congratulatory thoughts. He asked, "Paul, what were you thinking? Are you crazy? Do you know who you were talking to? That was *the* Robert Coleman!"

"Yup, and I think he really took my comments seriously. Praise God, huh?"

It wasn't until later that night when word had gotten back to Jerry, the conference director, that I began to grasp my arrogance and insensitivity. "Paul, what were you thinking? Are you crazy?" Jerry was a fellow first-year staff worker but much wiser.

I later apologized to Dr. Coleman, but he would hear none of it. He thanked me again for my input.

That episode quickly went into my all-time "If I could take this back I would in a heartbeat" file. But what I learned from Dr. Coleman and have never forgotten was his willingness to receive criticism, even from a brash, out-of-line young upstart. In future years, when young twenty-somethings would do likewise with me and my first impulse would be to defend my actions or blow them off, my mind would flash back to kind and gentle Robert Coleman.

Years later, I was speaking at a conference. A young staff worker, Betsy Wiley, approached me after my first talk and handed me a sheet of paper, filled with writing, front and back. "Thought this might help you, Paul," she said, and away she walked.

My immediate response as I read Betsy's critique was defensiveness. *Who does she think she is? I'm the conference speaker!* And then my mind flashed back to a scene years prior, to another conference speaker at another conference in northern Indiana. After swallowing a good dose of pride, I read on. *This is good stuff. She's right.*

I found Betsy and thanked her. I'm sure she was holding her breath. Not only was I the speaker, I was also her supervisor. From then on, whenever I spoke and Betsy was in the audience, I counted on her immediate, candid written feedback. Some of my talk files are full of her notes.

LEADERS SUBMIT TO OTHERS' LEADERSHIP AND AUTHORITY

Few things bring more fun and joy to our work than having a good boss. In my thirty years of working for InterVarsity, I've been privileged to have had several excellent supervisors who have profoundly shaped the way I lead. More than the reading of any book on leadership, observing how they led well provided grist for my own leadership. They weren't perfect. As I reflect back on them, each had major flaws but I could overlook their deficiencies because they had so much to offer me.

But what about bosses who drive us nuts with the way they lead, supervisors who seem clueless about even the most elementary parts of leadership? What then?

I've counseled or mediated in many "I can't take it anymore" supervisory situations. The reasons usually have fallen into one or more of the following categories:

- little mutual trust and respect, indispensable ingredients in any supervisory relationship
- unclear expectations for the position or role
- personality conflict
- character flaws
- differing styles of communication
- immoral behavior
- competition or jealousy
- don't trust their judgment and decision-making
- just plain don't like them

My advice in most of these cases was to not bail or ask to be transferred or look for a new supervisor. Sometimes, that's the only viable solution, but it should be explored only after looking for every possible way to make the current arrangement work. Why?

First, because Scripture urges us to do so: "Obey your leaders and submit to them, for they are keeping watch over your souls and will give an account. Let them do this with joy and not with sighing—for that would be harmful to you" (Heb 13:17 NRSV).

Second, it builds godly character in us like few things can. It especially improves our prayer life. Such hard relationships bring us to our knees, increasing our dependency on God alone.

Third, it can enable us to see things differently, if we are open. My way is not the only way or even the best way. Often as we pray God shows us our own flaws or ways we have damaged the working relationship. What was once just "their problem" now becomes "my problem" or "our problem."

Fourth, as we get used to seeing things differently, it may persuade us to change our own way of seeing and doing.

LEADERS WORK WITH PEOPLE OF DIFFERENT ETHNICITIES

One of the major challenges in the twenty-first century is tribalism, each people group staying to themselves and building up walls of protection. In his classic poem "Mending Wall" Robert Frost experiences rebuff from his neighbor who prefers a wall to developing a relationship with him, saying, "Good fences make good neighbours."

Frost yearns for a new reality for his generation: "Something there is that doesn't love a wall / That wants it down." In the end, to his dismay, the easier way of keeping the wall up prevails.

It is much easier and less complicated to surround ourselves with those who eat, dress, politick, believe and speak just like we do. Life becomes less conflicted and stressful and more predictable. It also becomes terribly boring and less challenging.

My personal "don't worry, be happy" dream world looks like this: live in California where I'm not such a minority; work alongside Asian American young adults, preferably fellow Japanese Americans; and drink lots of Peet's coffee.

God's "get real" world for me looks quite different. I have lived the past twenty-five years in Florida and Georgia, where the dominant minority is African Americans. We've lived in a predominantly black Atlanta neighborhood for fifteen years. Sam attended majority black schools from kindergarten through high school. We attend a Chinese American church. I play baseball in a league of 350 men of whom 95 percent are white. Since I joined eight years ago, I have been the only Asian American. When I come to bat, everyone knows who's up.

I'd be lying to say it's so cool living with this much diversity. When relationships are going well and I feel enriched by being with people ethnically different, *that* is cool. When there is tension and misunderstanding, cool is the last thing on my mind. Survival, retaliation or getting the heck out of Dodge are much more present.

From 1978 to 1997, I was a campus minister serving college students and staff in the Southeast. One of my primary reasons for coming south was to work in an environment where black and white racial issues were being dealt with on the surface and to see if I could be part of "the solution" to America's biggest social problem. What better place than the South?

By working in a region that honestly tried to wrestle with black and white issues, I received a Ph.D.'s worth of practical education. I used to chuckle that God had a great sense of humor sending a Californian Japanese American married to a white Mississippian to become the regional director in seven Southeastern states.

Well, usually I chuckled. Sometimes I groaned and moaned or kicked a tire in frustration. Black and white issues are always complex and often filled with pain and misunderstanding. On my better days as someone neither black nor white I thought of myself as a bridge person between the two races. On bleaker days, I cried out to God, "Why me? What am I doing here? This is *not* funny, God!"

Looking back, I wouldn't trade in those years, even the difficult ones. I would be pleased to live in Atlanta the rest of my life. This diversity, while sometimes nerve-wracking and exhausting, makes my life rich. It forces me to be open to ways of doing and thinking I normally would not consider. Sometimes I feel like a rubber band that is being stretched too far, ready to snap any minute. After the stretching eases, though, the rubber band contracts *but never to the same shape as before.* Living in such a diverse world has changed me. It has made me, I think, into a more thoughtful, openminded, compassionate person.

Learning to work with those of different ethnicities goes beyond political correctness. It is also "BC"—biblically correct. Revelation 7:9 informs us of the complexion of heaven:

> After this I [John] looked, and there was a great multitude that no one could count, from every nation, from all tribes and peoples and languages,

standing before the throne and before the Lamb, robed in white, with palm branches in their hands.

Apparently, heaven will not be filled with one celestial culture. There will remain the kind of racial and ethnic diversity we experience now. The question for us: Will we be ready for that much diversity or will it be uncomfortable and awkward because our worlds now are basically monocultural?

LEADERS EXPLORE HOW THEIR ETHNICITY INFORMS THEIR IDENTITY

Leadership in the twenty-first century inevitably means working with people of a variety of ethnicities. To do that well, it's important we understand not only others' ethnicity but we also learn about and embrace our own. To do that well takes time, candor and courage.

My wife, Margaret, does this as well as anyone I know. We joke now about how different our upbringings were. I am a third-generation Japanese American from California, a *sansei*, whose parents were imprisoned in America's World War II internment camps. Margaret is a white Deep Southerner from Mississippi, whose roots go back to Jamestown slave owners. In a college speech class, she gave a speech on patriotism; at the same time across the country, I marched in protest against some of the things done by our country.

One of her father's duties as a deacon in her Presbyterian church growing up was to greet visitors. If they were white, they could come on in. If they were black, they were not welcome and were directed to a black church. Growing up in deeply segregated Mississippi ingrained in Margaret a fear of blacks. When a student was killed at predominantly black Jackson State University in 1970, Margaret and her fellow freshmen at crosstown Belhaven College huddled in a dorm room, fearful of a reprisal on their all-white campus.

Five months later, she attended an InterVarsity-sponsored conference for students in Louisiana and Mississippi. At the time, InterVarsity was one of the few groups in Mississippi—Christian or secular—holding meetings for blacks and whites together.

At that conference, Margaret's small group leader was Elzilia, an African American student from New Orleans. It was Margaret's first experience being under the leadership of a black person. That simply didn't happen in Mississippi in 1970. When she reflected later on her experience and how much she had learned under Elzilia's leadership, she knew her worldview had changed forever.

When we started dating, she took my ethnicity seriously. I like to joke that she went to her library in Atlanta to check out all the books about Japanese Americans and immediately read them both. It was clear she was interested in me not *in spite* of my being Japanese American but partly because she saw how my ethnicity played a large role in who I was. That appealed to her.

When we had Sam, she vowed that he would not grow up fearing blacks like she had. We chose to live in a part of Atlanta that was integrated. When the neighborhood became predominantly black, we chose to stay rather than leave as many of our white neighbors had.

Margaret has taught Sam and me a great deal of African American culture and history. I know very few other nonblacks who have studied and read more about the African American experience than Margaret. Do I sound a little proud of her?

She has always been a student of her own ethnicity. She continues to read voraciously about what it means to be a Caucasian from the Deep South. As she reads, she has come to terms with white racism along with those parts of her culture for which she is justifiably proud. At times, she has to take a break from such study because it gets too intense and personal, but she always returns to it. Because racism infiltrates nooks and crannies of our being we never imagine existed, she continues to discover attitudes she needs to repent of—and she does.

Raising a biracial child is a formidable challenge. As parents, how do you affirm both cultures, without elevating one over the other? How do you help your child be 100 percent both rather than just 50 percent of each?

When Sam started preschool in Atlanta, Margaret asked the teacher if we could come in and teach a unit on Japanese culture. Her main goal? To help Sam gain an appreciation for his "Japanese side." As she was packing various Japanese memorabilia that she had collected over the years, she asked Sam if he would like to wear his *hapi* coat. He declined but she packed it just in case.

As we started the presentation, I watched Sam watch his classmates. As their interest grew, he went over to the box with his hapi coat and put it on. For the next several years, he would ask, "Mom, can we do the Japanese class again?"

Margaret lives out what I would like to see in Asian American leaders: a curiosity about other cultures, the courage to move out of one's comfort zone by making intentional, unnatural choices and a willingness to submit to the leadership of those considered inferior by one's own culture.

LEADERS MAKE A SUCCESS OF THOSE UNDER THEIR CARE

Eric and Dick met weekly to pray for each other. Dick was struggling in his supervision of a first-year employee, Damon. From Dick's perspective, Damon was immature, unreliable, impetuous and undisciplined. After hearing Dick out for several months, Eric leveled with him and said, "Dick, your problem is you are not willing to help Damon succeed."

When Dick mentioned this conversation to me, it hit me like a lightning bolt. That's exactly what Eric—my supervisor—had being doing for me! His goal was to make a success of me.

It got me reflecting on things Eric had done for me. I was Eric's administrative assistant for four years when he directed InterVarsity's media division, 2100 Productions. He could have easily dished off to me all the things he disliked doing. Rather his approach seemed to be "How can I utilize Paul in order to give him experiences and build qualities into his own life that will make him a better person and leader?"

When 2100 was asked to make a public presentation, Eric often asked me to represent us, even when it made more sense for him to go. He sought to build up my visibility and reputation, not his own.

He took calculated risks, giving me leadership roles that were beyond my experience. In my first year out of college, he appointed me team leader of a touring evangelistic media production, even though I was the youngest of the four members.

At the end of that year, he asked me to lead a six-week intern training project. I wince now when I recall assigning myself, age twenty-two, to be the Bible expositor for an entire week of the project. Eric didn't axe the idea but gave me some guidance along the way. I had only given maybe three or four talks prior to that week.

Perspective is everything. Eric saw that his role as my supervisor was not for me to help him succeed but for him to help me succeed. Many leaders embody the mantra, "It's all about me." For Eric, he clearly supervised me with "It's all about you, Paul—your success, your development."

I couldn't see it clearly then but I was seduced by power and influence. I took pride in being "Eric's right hand." Together we would dream what 2100 could become. I was getting very impressed with myself. Then one day Eric told me he was going to add two more people to his leadership team.

I was devastated. I had to take a sick day because it indeed sickened me. I didn't want to share my access to Eric with anyone else. Perceptively, Eric picked up what was going on with me. He loaned me a copy of C. S. Lewis's book *The Weight of Glory* and casually suggested I read a chapter called "The Inner Ring."

Rarely has something I've read changed my life as much as Lewis's short essay. In it he describes what happens when our desire to be an insider becomes our consuming ambition. Lewis was describing me, line by line! I was nailed and I knew it. I saw how my ambition was going to destroy me.

Bad patterns and habits don't change overnight. They die hard and not without a fight. It took a very bad experience for me to internalize what Eric was teaching me about biblical leadership.

During the fourth year that he supervised me, I asked Eric if we could hire someone to take on some of my job. I was told about Virginia, who was working in a high-powered role in the New York City political arena but wanted to work for a ministry organization. We brought her on to be my assistant.

I was impressed with her credentials. Unfortunately, I was more impressed with making a name for myself in InterVarsity. Virginia was going to help me do it better and quicker. I was full of ambition and full of my-self. Without articulating it, I thought her job was to make me succeed. We actually started out great. She brought energy, passion and great talent. She had that Big Apple life of the party disposition.

I was shocked about eight months into her job when she handed me her resignation. "I can't work for you," she said. "You're impossible to work for."

Shock turned into disbelief. *I can't be that bad,* I thought. *How dare she!* Disbelief turned into anger. *I can't afford to have this on my record.* Anger in time turned into shame.

Years later I finally asked myself, "What did I do wrong to let this happen?" I didn't like what I remembered. I had given Virginia assignments that would free me for high visibility roles. I rarely thought about ways to develop her as a person. I didn't allow her to get inside my head to understand my decisions and choices.

About ten years later, I ran into Virginia. We had not really communicated since her resignation, except a few awkward hellos at social gatherings. I told her my distorted view of leadership had caught her in the crosshairs of my misfires. "Virginia, I'm sorry I was such a poor supervisor to you," I said. "I hope you can forgive me." She did.

Blowing it badly, like I did with Virginia, drove me to prayer—to repent and ask for forgiveness. When I came to a place where I could ask God, "Now what, boss?" invariably, he would point me to his word for direction and to the One who got it right.

6   JESUS BEATS THE WARLORDS

When I'm in the market for a car or computer or any other large item, I don't hesitate: I'm there at <www.consumerreports.org> looking for *the* best buy. For me, two unforgivable sins are paying retail and buying a real lemon because I didn't do my homework.

I don't want the model that blows the competition away in its outward appearance only to fall apart thirteen months later—a month after the warranty expires—due to inferior parts or poor workmanship. I want the very best my budget can handle. I can't afford to be taken for an economic ride. I'm not rolling in enough green to have that luxury.

When I look for Asian America's best model of a pretty good leader, I don't need to go online. The very best is an arm's length away. His vita is the New Testament. That's where I can find all I need to know about our best leader: the one and only Jesus.

I want a leader who not only stands up to the competition, I need one who shuts them down and slams the door. When I read the Gospels, I find the one who stands up to the "competition" I face daily as an Asian American.

The competition for our allegiance is fierce. It comes from a variety of sources who beckon with powerful and alluring voices.

SONG OF THE SIRENS

In Greek mythology, the Sirens, daughters of the sea god Phorcys, had such sweet voices that sailors who heard their songs were lured into grounding their boats on the rocks on which the daughters sang. The

Greek hero Odysseus was able to pass their island in safety because he plugged the ears of his companions with wax and had himself firmly bound to the mast of the ship so that he could hear the songs without danger.

According to another legend, the band of heroes called the Argonauts escaped the Sirens because the musician Orpheus, who was on board their ship, the *Argo,* sang so sweetly that he drowned out the song of the daughters.

As Asian Americans, sometimes we need to plug our ears to voices that allure us. If there's another lesson to learn from dealing with our own Sirens, it's clear we cannot escape them on our own. As Odysseus had his companions tie him to the mast and the Argonauts depended on Orpheus to sing a sweeter song, we need the help of others.

That "sweeter song" for us is the life and teachings of Jesus. When we fully devote ourselves to his song, his good news, we can escape the Sirens in our lives. It's not easy, and at times the allure *will* lure us, the music *is* going to get us, but our Orpheus can and will prevail.

Who are the Asian American Sirens? Who constantly steps into the ring with Jesus vying for our allegiance? I am aware of four such Sirens. Undoubtedly there are more and as time goes by, newcomers will rise in prominence.

JESUS VERSUS PARENTS WHO ACT LIKE GOD

Helen Zia reflects on her family life:

> In our household it was understood that no one should ever disobey, contradict, or argue with the patriarch [father], who, in the Confucian hierarchy, is a stand-in for God. My mother, and of course the children, were expected to obey God absolutely. This system occasionally broke down when my mother and father quarreled, usually about my father's rigid expectations of us. But in the end, God always seemed to win.[1]

The issue here is the proper place of authority.

Parents are God's unique gift to us. Without them, we wouldn't be here. That in itself is enough for which to be eternally grateful. But it doesn't stop there. Without their constant care, who knows what wrong turns we might have taken? For some of us, that's a frightening thought. Without their financial help, our college diploma might be less prestigious or perhaps nonexistent. Without those generous checks, we might still be paying off college loans until Jesus comes back.

At Asian American weddings I see all of this gratitude reach its apex and flow freely. Somewhere between the vows and walking down the aisle as a married couple, the couple stops to acknowledge each set of parents. They share tokens like flowers and words only meant for the other to hear.

I confess I've yet to make it past this part of an Asian American wedding without crying. Even the young groom, trained to restrain emotions, weeps. It's as if for a few brief moments, all the shared difficulties of the past are swept aside and only the good memories surface to make it a Kodak moment. I savor those moments because I've heard enough blood-sweat-tears parent-child stories to make me pound my fists in frustration and anger, usually at the parents.

Thankfully, not all Asian American parents are like this. However, if you are a child of pressuring parents, you have three choices. One, you can bail. You refuse to follow "the plan." Like a running back, you straight-arm your parents whenever they attempt to tackle you with their hopes and dreams for you. Or two, when they act like God, you bow your knee. You fulfill their will for your life. In your heart, you pray, "Yes, Lord Ma, yes, Lord Pa."

Choice number three, you invite Jesus to lead you down the slender trail that leads to a rich life. You cling to his promises, like in Matthew 19:29-30:

> And everyone who has left houses or brothers or sisters or father or mother or children or fields for my sake will receive a hundred times as much and will inherit eternal life. But many who are first will be last, and many who are last will be first.

At the same time, in choosing Jesus, you shudder at passages like Matthew 10:34-38:

Do not suppose that I have come to bring peace to the earth. I did not come to bring peace, but a sword. For I have come to turn "a man against his father, a daughter against her mother, a daughter-in-law against her mother-in-law—a man's enemies will be the members of his own household."

Anyone who loves his father or mother more than me is not worthy of me; anyone who loves his son or daughter more than me is not worthy of me; and anyone who does not take his cross and follow me is not worthy of me.

You shudder but obey because verse 39 follows: "Whoever finds his life will lose it, and whoever loses his life for my sake will find it."

You risk even the blessing of your parents because you want to find life.

"DAD, MAY I PLEASE HAVE YOUR BLESSING?"

My senior year at Cal Poly-San Luis Obispo was coming to a close when my family came to visit me during Poly Royal, our big springtime weekend "country fair on a college campus." I had just been asked to join the staff of InterVarsity. My parents had not yet asked what my plans were after graduation, just months away. They were always good at giving their children space to make their own decisions. But I didn't just want space. I wanted more.

Sunday came and I still had said nothing. I knew I had to spill the beans but was terrified. My parents were Buddhists. Just prior to their hopping in the car to head back home, Captain Courageous sucked it up.

"Can we talk, Dad?" I asked.

We went to a back bedroom at my Auntie Shizuko's house in San Luis Obispo and closed the door. We sat side by side on the bed. Serious father-son conversations were rare for us. I took a deep breath and told him my plans.

Then I went for the downs: "Dad, may I have your blessing?" His head dropped. He said nothing. Finally, with his head still down, he quietly said, "You need to do what you need to do."

That should have been enough but I was desperate for his approval. Again: "Dad, may I *please* have your blessing?" Head still down, one more time: "You need to do what you need to do." He got up and left the room. Minutes later, my family drove off.

That was my Black Sunday, one of the darkest days of my life. I had a meeting that afternoon in the student union. I went there early and sat in one of the sofas in the nearly deserted building and wept. The unique pain of disappointing the most important person in my life wracked my entire body.

I cried not only for myself but also for Dad. I was Number One Son, the place of highest honor and responsibility in Asian families. With this vocational choice, I was not going to be a good role model for my three younger siblings. He was not going to be able to brag about me with his friends and coworkers. Dad was also a leader in the Japanese American community. For the first time, I was able to see how my choice would not only bring family stress to me. It would also publicly shame him.

Two months later, my family was back on campus for my graduation. The morning of our afternoon graduation, a senior brunch was held for graduates and their families. I was able to reserve a table near the dais for Mom, Dad, my siblings, my aunt and her daughter. Over one thousand of my classmates' friends and family were present.

The high point of the program was the presentation of the Chester G. Young Award. Dr. Young had been executive vice-president at Cal Poly for years and was college president Robert Kennedy's closest friend. Dr. Young had died earlier that year. Dr. Kennedy wanted to honor him by selecting the outstanding graduating senior "who most embodied the qualities of Chet Young."

It seemed clear that Robin Baggett was the hands-down choice. Student body president, all-conference catcher, honor student, pre-law, a good guy. Robin and I had become close friends that year. I was pleased his accomplishments would be honored.

When Dr. Kennedy said my name and not Robin's, I was stunned. I stumbled to the dais to receive the award. As I said a few clumsy words, I looked down at my father. I watched tears roll down his cheeks. It was only the second time in my life I recall him crying. The first was when his beloved boss and mentor died from a sudden heart attack when I was ten.

What did the tears mean? Certainly they were tears of joy and pride. But were they also mingled with tears of disappointment? Of the three thousand graduates that day, his son was singled out as outstanding. Look what he's doing with his life! Throwing it away by entering ministry! Christian ministry!

That senior brunch happened nearly thirty years ago. I am still on the staff of InterVarsity. I have ministered these years without the blessing of my father or mother. What I have ministered with is the fulfillment of Matthew 19:29-30, fathers, mothers, brothers and sisters, a hundred times over.

Do I regret my choice to enter ministry without my father's blessings? I do not. After that bedside rejection, I have never looked back. Has the absence of his blessing made ministry harder? Without question. I would have been a better, freer leader knowing he was behind me, but the family of God has always been there for me. I couldn't have lasted more than a year or two without them.

I chose Jesus' wishes for my life over those of my parents'. I am convinced I am a better son for making this choice and living with its consequences. Jesus was right: "Whoever finds his life will lose it, and whoever loses his life for my sake will find it." I have an unbelievably rich life.

I want to be clear—my choice should not be everyone's. For each, Jesus leads uniquely. I have counseled some Asian American young adults to take the same road I chose; with others, it seemed right to follow the wishes of their parents. There is not one correct answer that we all follow. Rather, we follow him who knows what's best for us and we trust him one step at a time. Our default mode should be to seek obedience before disobedience.

As a college sophomore, I had registered to attend InterVarsity's triennial Urbana missions convention. My travel plans were set. Three days before I was to depart, Doug, my staff worker, called me at my folks' house to make sure I was still good to go. I had asked permission several months before and had received it.

"Let me check with Dad," I said and put Doug on hold. I'm glad I did because Dad said, "I don't want you to go. You shouldn't be spending your money on something not related to your education." I got back on the phone with Doug and told him Dad's response. "We'll cover all your expenses, Paul," Doug replied.

Back to Dad a second time put him on the spot. It was clear he didn't want me to go but couldn't come up with a logical reason. I could keep stringing him out with silence or I could bail him out.

"Dad, if you don't want me to go, I won't go," I said. With a surprised look, he quietly said, "I don't want you to go."

"Doug, I'm sorry but I can't go." Doug was disappointed but he understood.

The rest of Christmas break had a different feel. I sensed Dad respected me a bit more. I realized there would be many more great conferences to attend but I had only one father for the rest of my life.

JESUS VERSUS HARVARD

Is Jesus down on Harvard? No. It would be inconsistent with the character of God to dismiss one of the better institutional developers of the mind. When Jesus told us to love God with the fullness of our minds, I'm sure Harvard was in his blueprints as a great place to help some do that.

What Jesus is down on is the exaltation of any place or anybody. Harvard, Stanford, the University of Michigan—any of our finest learning institutions can be the illegitimate focus of our affections.

Asian Americans are known for their unrequited love affair of anything Ivy. Susan Cho Van Riesen, in *Following Jesus Without Dishonoring Your Parents*, tells of some Korean American parents who named their children Harvard and Yale in order to give them a leg up on other high school seniors come college application time. (We should be glad Slippery Rock University and Ursinus College aren't Ivies.) Let's not lay all blame on parents. We, too, succumb to brand name schools.

My high school grade point average of 3.0 and 932 SAT score kept me out of any top-rung school. I literally fell asleep taking the SAT because I had partied too hard and too late the night before! I settled for Cal Poly, a part of the California state college and university system. My education there was superb and I am proud to be a Poly alumnus.

After I graduated and non-Californians would ask where I went to school, I would often watch their eyebrows lift as their "Oh . . ." communicated inappropriate awe and respect. After a while, I figured out what was going through their minds: *Wow, he went to Cal Tech; he must be really bright!* I chose not to clarify their thinking. Years later, Cal Poly—my school—became increasingly difficult to get into and would rank high in *U.S. News and World Report*'s "Best Colleges" listing. Then when the eyebrows lifted, my little ego-jacking charade was a tad more legitimate.

I find it hard to quit this game. Recently, Donna Dong, a veteran campus ministry coworker, and I were driving onto the Stanford campus. I was to speak at Stanford Christian Fellowship's weekly meeting. As we looked for parking amongst the Acuras, Lexuses and assorted SUVs, I could feel the pressure building up inside.

Finally I blurted out to Donna, "Boy, speaking at Stanford sure intimidates me! I'm just a state college guy!" What I didn't say but was feeling was *Do I have anything to say to Stanford students?* and *What if they find out I went to Cal Poly? Will they snicker then blow me off?* To my surprise and comfort, Donna, a Cal Berkeley graduate, exclaimed, "Gee, you too? Speaking here intimidates me too! I'm glad it's not just me!" Sharing our "We're at Stanford!" insecurities was comforting.

As Asian American leaders, we must demystify education's designer labels and stop bowing our knee toward Cambridge and Palo Alto. Appropriate respect is healthy, but giving them godlike status is sacrilegious. I confess I treat a Harvard student differently than one at Bunker Hill Community College. *They must be special,* goes my thinking, *they made it into Harvard.* That is wrong and I need to repent of my elitism. The Ivys and almost-Ivys are not the best places for all of us to be educated. If all higher education institutions are God's means of growing our minds, I need to grow in my respect for all of them.

Watching Jesus interact with the educational elite of his day, the Pharisees, gives me a healthier view of education. He denounced their preoccupation with titles and honors: "Everything they do is done for men to see: . . . they love to be greeted in the marketplaces and to have men call them 'Rabbi.' . . . The greatest among you will be your servant. For whoever exalts himself will be humbled, and whoever humbles himself will be exalted" (Mt 23:5, 7, 11-12).

What truly irritated Jesus was the hypocrisy of the Pharisees. He ends his tirade with a series of seven woes to them, calling them hypocrites (Mt 23:13-32). For Jesus, the purpose of education was to help people love God with all their minds. It was not to leverage favors and prestige and create structures based on knowledge, wealth and family position. When Jesus slams the door on the Pharisees, he calls them "You snakes! You brood of vipers!"

What on the surface sounds awfully harsh and vicious may be well-deserved. Much is asked of leaders and they are judged by a higher standard because of their influence and power.

JESUS VERSUS YIN AND YANG

By nature I am a yin and yang kind of guy. I find that circle with the entwined black wave—white dot and white wave—black dot strangely comforting. It conjures up images of Mr. Miyagi in *The Karate Kid,* a nice blend of serenity and intensity. I want a life that includes both growing bonsais and helping Daniel-sans whoop up on large guys (figuratively speaking, of course). I want to "wax on, wax off" forever.

For years, I sought a balanced life:

- time for work—time for play
- time for family—time for friends
- relationships with Christians—friendships with non-Christians
- being with Asians—non-Asians
- making sure I took days off after intense weekend conferences
- having no conflicted relationships

WHAT IS YIN AND YANG?

Yin and yang are opposite and complementary forces in Chinese thought, from Chinese words meaning "shaded" and "sunny." Beginning in the early 4th century BC Chinese philosophers wrote about yin and yang in terms of the environment, especially the shaded and sunny sides of a hill. By the end of that century yin became associated with everything dark, moist, receptive, earthy, and female, whereas yang was bright, dry, active, heavenly, and male. Yin and yang were believed to combine in various proportions to produce all the different objects in the universe.

Chinese philosophers stressed the importance of balance between the two to ensure social and political harmony. Rebellion, floods, and disease were said to be caused by an imbalance of yin and yang. Fortune-tellers and doctors in China and later in Japan advised governments and individuals on ways to restore harmony in relationship to yin and yang.[2]

Without giving it much thought, I equated such balance with godliness. But Jesus wasn't a yin and yang kind of savior. The writer Mark especially captures this as he chronicles Jesus' life. Balance and harmony don't seem to be intrinsic to his teaching nor central to his lifestyle. Rather, *passion* seems to drive his life. Passion for doing his Father's will. Passion for the lost. Passion for the rights of those marginalized by the powers that be. Passion for damaged people to experience healing and wholeness that only God can bring. Passion for purity of thoughts and actions.

Such passion drives him to begin the first month and a half of public ministry not in a classroom but risking his life with wild animals on an empty stomach. It drives him to ask grown men to abandon vocation and families in order to spend time with him. His hatred of evil is so strong that he probably bankrupts a wealthy farmer when he sends demons into two thousand pigs and over a cliff. He rebukes the wind, rubs his own spit on the face of a deaf-mute to bring sight and hearing. He talks to a fig tree.

When he gets "carried away" with his ministry to the point where people think he has an evil spirit and his own family members come to take him home, he blows them off. He skips meals, loses sleep and has to flex on his quiet times in order to fulfill the mission of his Father. His passion drives him to people of the "wrong" heritage and color.

Such passion keeps Jesus up at night and drives him to pray for hours on end. It moves him to weep when friends die. This passion provokes him to anger when religious leaders put policy over people. When they can't control him, they conspire to assassinate him. And because of his overriding passion to see his Father's will done, he lets them do it.

The more I am willing to let Jesus penetrate my yin and yang world, the more I am driven by passion, not balance. What is good for one's blood pressure doesn't necessarily rattle the gates of hell or grow the kingdom of God. At my funeral, I'll flip in my grave if someone eulogizes me, "He lived such a balanced life."

Where yin and yang often impacts Asian American leaders is in the area of conflict. When we disagree, we think of every way possible that doesn't force us to disagree directly. We give in before we will say, "Sarah, no way!" When our personalities clash, better for me to back off and even

bow out than work out how our differences can be optimized. Just thinking of these scenarios causes us to reach for the Pepto-Bismol bottle.

Leaning on the everlasting arms of yin and yang also takes away our willingness to call people to risk hugely. Jim Collins and Jerry Porras in *Built to
Last: Successful Habits of Visionary Companies* use the yin and yang paradigm to show how highly successful companies combine yin (preserve the
core values) and yang (stimulate growth). [3] They offer five ways to stimulate growth, all of them quite risky. The catchiest one they call BHAGs: Big
Hairy Audacious Goals. To have a BHAG is to risk hugely. As Asian Americans we are not known for our BHAGs. We prefer Moderate Fuzzy Attain-
able Goals. We're superb at doing yin; it's yang we could work on.

As I work with Asian American college students and young adults, I
see an increasing hunger to have their lives count for more than five bed-
rooms with three baths and a killer portfolio. When I talk about *living la
vida loca*—the crazy life of the kingdom inaugurated by Jesus—the lights
always go on in at least several pairs of eyes. At the same time, of course,
I see some lights dim just as the rich young ruler's did when Jesus told
him what following him would cost. But ten years ago, I saw few eyes
lighting up. I'm heartened for this generation.

I love this quote from novelist Pearl S. Buck, who lived in China for
many years: "The young do not know enough to be prudent, and therefore
they attempt the impossible—and achieve it, generation after generation."

Let me point out there is a difference between passion for God's ways
and things like stupidity, flakiness, irresponsibility and poor taste. We
should still pay our bills, call Mom on Mother's Day, try to lose the extra
pounds we gained over the holidays and root for our favorite team. Those
things matter; we're just not going to let them drive who we are. We're not
plumb dumb-crazy, we're just passionate for God and his ways. It's a huge
difference though not everyone will see it that way. So be it!

JESUS: THE BEST MODEL FOR ASIAN AMERICAN LEADERS

Not only does Jesus trump the "warlords," he offers Asian American leaders so much more than the competition. Throughout the Gospels, he does
things and relates to people in ways in which we can identify. Been there,

done that, still do that. He also does things we can't imagine doing, which elongates our comfort zone. On our own gumption, there's no way we could go there. But when we are empowered by the Holy Spirit, we experience the truth of Jesus' words to the disciples: "Very truly, I tell you, the one who believes in me will also do the works that I do and, in fact, will do greater works than these, because I am going to the Father" (Jn 14:12). As we step forward to lead, what can we count on from Jesus?

JESUS HAD *OMOIYARI*

Takie Sugiyama Lebra writes in *Japanese Patterns of Behavior*:

> For the Japanese, empathy (or *omoiyari*) ranks high among the virtues considered indispensable for one to be really human, morally mature, and deserving of respect.
>
> I am even tempted to call Japanese culture an omoiyari culture. Omoiyari refers to the ability and willingness to feel what others are feeling, to vicariously experience the pleasure or pain that they are undergoing, and to help them satisfy their wishes.[4]

While *omoiyari* is characteristic of Japanese people, it also exists in other Asian cultures. Rebecca Pippert writes of a man full of *omoiyari* in *Out of the Saltshaker*:

> Jesus was profoundly compassionate. He cared deeply and was not afraid to show it. He was profoundly committed to setting people free and making them whole. He touched people at the deepest level. He wanted to heal not only blindness and leprosy but also the things that prevented joy and beauty and freedom and justice.

She goes on to describe his compassion:

> His feelings were no deeper than his practical concern. He healed Jairus' daughter, and at the moment of this stupendous miracle he simply told them to get her something to eat. His care was consistent. Never flashy, sometimes almost quiet. Even after his death, Jesus demonstrated the very same care. If I had been resurrected, I would have rented the Coliseum and hired the London Philharmonic Choir to sing the "Hallelujah Chorus." But in one postresurrection account we find Jesus making the disciples a little breakfast![5]

Jesus can take this natural bent we have toward being *omoiyari* people and enrich it with the fruit of the Spirit: love, joy, peace, patience, kindness, generosity, faithfulness, gentleness and self-control. When that blending happens, we'll attract people like moths to a light.

JESUS KNEW WHAT WOMEN WANT

In Jesus' day, women wanted to be respected and taken seriously, free to minister and not regarded as sex toys or property. Some things don't change.

Asian American men have not always treated women well. The rap often goes like this: Asian American men don't communicate their deep feelings—if we truly have any. We treat women like property. We don't like to do "unmanly" household chores. And under our cool façade, Asian American men are angry—at never measuring up to white men, getting beaten out by them for the most desirable Asian American women, being scripted by American society as techno-mad geeks who adore their cars and personal digital assistants.

We could argue with this critique ad inifinitum. A better approach would be to look at the one who got it right with women.

Jesus was amazing with women. They leaped over cultural and religious hurdles just to be around him. When he taught, he often used women as examples, never as the butt of jokes but as people with value and dignity. This wasn't lost on his crowds of listeners. Neither was his advocacy for women who found themselves entrapped by a male-favoring culture.

Jesus challenged the prevailing views on divorce that hung women out to dry (Lk 16:18). Rather than see a crippled woman spend another day in pain, he healed her on the sabbath, provoking the ire of the religious leaders (Lk 13:10). He respected their personhood by addressing mixed crowds instead of segregating women from men and addressing them separately or not at all. In crowds, women risked the ridicule and condemnation of men in order to gain his ear (Lk 11:27).

His personal interactions with women were consistent with what he taught publicly. Rather than parlay his platform and growing fame to gain sexual favors or take advantage of women in other ways, Jesus never flirted or hit on them. His no-games relational style created freedom for women to approach him, unique in the culture of the day. He risked being misunderstood when he physically touched women in order to heal them.

Some were so bold as to touch him physically to be healed from lifelong infirmities (Mk 5:27). At times, he risked the cultural double whammy of relating to women from cultures despised by his fellow Jews (Jn 4; Mk 7:24; Mt 15:21).

He was unafraid to let his emotions show. My favorite verse in all the Gospels is John 11:35: "Jesus wept." When faced with the death of his close friend Lazarus and the grief it brought the family, he didn't start preparing an appropriate funeral homily. He wept. He cried. He probably bawled his eyes out with Lazarus's sisters, Martha and Mary.

When Mary confronted Jesus with, "Lord, if you had been here, my brother would not have died," she spit out the words with a controlled maelstrom of bitterness, anger, frustration and resentment. I'm glad for Mary and Martha (and of course for Lazarus) that Jesus eventually brings his friend back to life, but I'm more touched that Jesus cried for his friend. I find it easier to do godly things to help people but much more difficult to feel and absorb the pain of my friends.

His male pride didn't keep him from receiving from women. Joanna, a highly visible wife of a Roman public official, Susanna and many other women both traveled with Jesus as he ministered from town to town and also helped pick up the tab for expenses (Lk 8:2).

And as he hung on the cross, it wasn't Peter, James and John with him, those we might expect to be with him at his time of greatest need. Mark makes it clear for us:

> Some women were watching from a distance. Among them were Mary Magdalene, Mary the mother of James the younger and of Joses, and Salome. In Galilee these women had followed him and cared for his needs. Many other women who had come up with him to Jerusalem were also there. (Mk 15:39-41)

JESUS MADE SPACE FOR THE MARGINALIZED

Who lacks a public voice today? Who gets shoved to society's edges and can't shove back?

Among others, it's those without financial means, those of the "wrong" color and those too young or too old. To lead responsibly is to make sure the voiceless get a fair hearing.

Jesus always made the forgotten feel unforgettable. In a culture where children were undervalued, they flocked to him because he found them delightful. When he described true faith, he told adults to see things through the eyes of a child. When adults hushed kids up and shooed them away, Jesus put children on his lap and gave them his undivided attention. When I am asked to assess a potential leader, I always look for how they treat children.

Racial purity was preached from the pulpits of Jesus' day. Judaism had few escape clauses that allowed for interracial mixing. Non-Jews were "dogs." Jesus led by example and began breaking down the racial walls of hostility.

> Leaving that place, Jesus withdrew to the region of Tyre and Sidon. A Canaanite woman from that vicinity came to him, crying out, "Lord, Son of David, have mercy on me! My daughter is suffering terribly from demon-possession."
>
> Jesus did not answer a word. So his disciples came to him and urged him, "Send her away, for she keeps crying out after us."
>
> He answered, "I was sent only to the lost sheep of Israel."
>
> The woman came and knelt before him. "Lord, help me!" she said. He replied, "It is not right to take the children's bread and toss it to their dogs."
>
> "Yes, Lord," she said, "but even the dogs eat the crumbs that fall from their masters' table."
>
> Then Jesus answered, "Woman, you have great faith! Your request is granted." And her daughter was healed from that very hour. (Mt 15:21-28)

This was not an isolated incident that we can easily skip over. It happened time and again, with the Samaritan woman, the centurion in Capernaum. Jesus was clearly making a point about the composition of the kingdom.

Asian American Christians are often guilty of refusing to mix with non-Asian "dogs." Sometimes we are afraid of being contaminated by too much contact which might even lead to producing "mongrels."

Defying those with zero racial tolerance takes immense courage from leaders. Defending racial purity brings out the very worse in people. Fine and reasonable people can suddenly turn ugly and irrational when pushed to interact with those from races they despise. It can touch a raw nerve that sets off seismic reactions that make other displays of evil look downright tame.

Jesus' concern didn't stop with those ethnically different. He had a deep concern for the poor and those rendered powerless by the government and religious establishment.

THE ONE, THE ONLY, THE BEST

Sirens allure us. Their songs will change in tune, melody and lyrics but they will never go away. We must pump up the volume of our Orpheus— Jesus, the one, the only, the best—for only his sweet song can drown out his pretenders.

New Biblical Paradigms for Leadership

Moses and Esther

_____

_____

A̲sk Western evangelicals who after Jesus is the most influential shaper of the Christian faith, and most would answer the apostle Paul. And rightly so. Paul's story in Acts holds us spellbound by his miraculous turnaround, bravery and commitment to Jesus. His letters to friends and churches impress us with how his theological imprint has endured over time and continues to shape and guide the church.

But all of us, Asian American or not, are poorer if we don't allow the whole of Scripture shape our lives individually and corporately. We have other role models to follow besides only Jesus and Paul.

NEW BIBLICAL PARADIGMS

As Asian Americans we readily identify with those in Scripture who

- are ethnic minorities
- relocate to a new locale and adopt a new culture
- undergo prejudice and racism
- lead as minorities in the majority culture
- are bilingual, favoring one tongue over the other
- have a high view of family

Additionally, those of us who marry out and raise biracial children will identify with interracial marriages found in Scripture.

Moses and Esther are role models for Asian Americans, not that they did everything right but because we can identify with much of what they encountered and wrestled with. Most important, they were ordinary people who exercised extraordinary leadership when empowered by the God of surprises.

MOSES

Even before day one, Moses was in trouble. He was born an Israelite, part of a thriving minority community in Egypt. As the Hebrew population in Egypt flourished, Egypt's leader Pharaoh was threatened. He knew that the Hebrews' occupation of border territory made it convenient to defect to a neighboring enemy. Pharaoh feared that an attack from an Israelite-neighboring country alliance could end the Egyptian empire. He responded by consolidating the area into two store-cities (housing arms and supplies for defense and attack), enslaving the Israelites and instituting the slaughter of male babies.

Two certain Hebrew midwives chose to exercise civil disobedience. They refused to kill the male babies and lied when confronted by Pharaoh. God blessed them by giving them their own families. When Pharaoh discovered this, he escalated the slaughter. The world Moses was about to enter would be void of a generation of Jewish males.

While Moses' playmates were being exterminated, his life was spared. Upon his birth, his mother hid him for three months. Then through divine family planning, Moses was adopted by the very daughter of Pharaoh but spent his baby and toddler years raised by his own family. Knowing he was only on loan to them likely in-

---

MOSES: SOUTHEAST ASIAN PROTOTYPE?

Many of Moses' early experiences are shared by Southeast Asian Americans who came to the United States in the latter part of the twentieth century:

- *born in a foreign country*

- *escaped the holocaust of a whole generation of male peers*

- *owed his life to courageous women who performed acts of civil disobedience*

- *had an Asian American-style mother (strongly parented as a young child)*

- *bilingual, bicultural "1.5" upbringing*

- *adopted into and raised in the mainstream culture*

- *name changed to fit into a new culture*

- *forced to choose one ethnic identity over the other*

- *chosen by God to lead a people group of which he was not truly a part*

tensified their parenting and nurturing. He may have been as old as four when Moses' mother stopped nursing him.[1] When Moses' final adoption is transacted, he is a youngster deeply loved and cared for by his family.

When I try to picture Moses' mother, I see one who resembles many Asian American mothers, fiercely devoted to their children's long-term well-being. She went to great lengths to ensure her baby wouldn't die. She was a daring tactician, figuring out a way to have him raised by those with the means to bring him up well. She echoes Asian American mothers who work themselves to the bone to send their son to Harvard, who would even be willing to live with him during finals, doing his laundry and cooking, so he could be totally devoted to studying and doing well. In later years, we see the same tenacity in Moses the leader.

Korean Americans use the term 1.5 to describe those born in Korea who immigrated to America as children with their families. They are squarely of two cultures—Korean and American, belonging partly to both and fully to neither. Other Asian American groups have borrowed that label to describe similar experiences. Moses was clearly 1.5.

Following his adoption as a toddler, he is renamed Moses by strangers, which in Egyptian means "to draw out," perhaps "to draw out of the water." He must have wondered, *Why do they keep calling me Moses? My name is* ____. (We're not told what his parents named him at birth.)

His adoptive mother, though the daughter of a despot, has a soft spot for children and likely raised him with love and devotion. Moses becomes a blend of both Hebrew and Egyptian cultures. He is exposed to and probably asked to worship Egyptian gods. He was bilingual, knowing both the Hebrew and Egyptian languages.

At age forty (Acts 7:23-29), Moses faces a situation that clarifies and defines his ethnic identity. Seeing a fight break out between an Egyptian and a Hebrew, he asks the question to which there is no one right answer. It's the question that every "hyphenated American" hopes is never asked of them: "Who am I? Am I Egyptian or am I Hebrew? Hebrew or Egyptian?"

Action—not ideology or hypothetical discussions over double lattes—defines our true beliefs. *Moses, who will you side with forever?*

"Who will you side with?" is the same question posed in early 1943 to young Japanese American men in America's World War II internment camps. The United States asked the very men they had incarcerated if they would now fight on behalf of their country. These men were asked to declare their loyalty to the United States when each was forced to answer two questions:

"Are you willing to serve in the armed forces of the United States on combat duty, wherever ordered?"

"Will you swear unqualified allegiance to the United States of America and faithfully defend the United States from any or all attack by foreign or domestic forces, and foreswear any form of allegiance or obedience to the Japanese emperor, to any other foreign government, power or organization?"

These controversial and loaded questions brought raw emotions to the surface to these American citizens. The powerful Japanese American Citizens League endorsed the drafting of Japanese Americans for military service as a way to show their allegiance to the United States. These two questions frequently split up families, with one son saying "Yes, yes," the other "No, no."

In the end, most of them said yes to both. The 282 who responded "No" to the first question were imprisoned for three years. For them, they felt it was unconstitutional for the U.S. government to strip them of their rights and then draft them. They would only enlist if their civil rights were restored and their families first released from the internment camps.

Those who responded negatively to both questions were branded the "No-No Boys" and considered traitors even though very little disloyalty was ever displayed.

In 1947, President Harry Truman pardoned the 282, but it wasn't until 2002 that the JACL apologized for originally calling them "cowards, traitors and subversives."

When Moses sides with the Hebrew and kills the Egyptian, he knows it is a decision fraught with consequences. To have killed the Hebrew or done nothing would have kept Moses on the safe course, enjoying all the benefits of Egyptian royalty. To kill one from his adopted culture immediately drew a line in the sand. After thirtysomething years, he crosses from Egyptian to Hebrew in his self-identity. World history literally turns on his choice.

With that choice, Moses loses everything. He gives up the life of royalty. Any hope of inheritance dissolves. He nearly loses his life at Pharaoh's own hand. As he flees Egypt, he leaves everything but knows this: "I, Moses, am a Hebrew."

Here's what made Moses' choice different from that of the young Japa-

QUESTIONS FOR US FROM MOSES' LIFE

Reading about Moses raises questions about our own leadership development as Asian Americans:

- *Clearly, Moses' "sovereign foundations" profoundly shaped him. In what ways can you likewise see how God "set the table" of your life before you were born? In what ways were you profoundly shaped in your childhood and adolescence?*

- *Moses must have felt torn being a Hebrew raised in Egyptian culture. In what ways do you feel uncomfortable in American culture? When you're in an Asian setting? Which culture feels most like home for you?*

- *Moses had an unusual past for a person called to be such a leader. What about your past prepared you for leadership? What burning bush or kairos moments in your life did you have? How did God prove himself to you during those moments?*

- *What in your past has worked against your becoming a good*

leader? How might something you've always thought of as a detriment somehow enhance your leadership?

- *In what ways was your family a positive force behind your development as a leader? What things did your parents or siblings do that helped shape who you are today? Conversely, did they do anything that had a negative impact on your development as a leader?*

- *What elements of your Asian heritage impacted your growth as a leader? What elements of Confucianism help in leadership development? Hinder?*

- *Moses responds to God by moving his family to an unknown place. What were the circumstances of your ancestors coming to the United States? Was it a smooth or difficult move?*

- *God is asking of Moses a huge task. What huge tasks has God asked of you that you objected to and felt overwhelmed by? How* nese American men in 1943. The worst it could cost them was more severe prison conditions and family conflict. For Moses, it was life or death.

Growing up, Moses was exposed to the harsh living conditions of Hebrew slaves. At some point he had to wonder, where were his Hebrew male peers? He eventually must have realized that his "grandpa" Pharaoh

did they turn out? How did this affect your faith and trust in God?

- *What are some ways you are unable to be used by God in an Asian culture because of your inability to relate to that culture? Conversely, in what ways are you unable to be used in the dominant culture because of your "Asianness?" Who are the Aarons in your life—those who can help you be more effective in both cultures?*

- *Reflect on Moses' "leadership development track" in Exodus 5-10. Watch how God interacts with him, how Moses responds, the challenges that push him to grow and develop, his maturation as a leader willing to confront authority, his struggles with his personal shortcomings. At what points do you see Moses and Aaron stepping out in deeper trust in God? Reflecting on your own life, name the times you stepped out in faith and how God met you.*

- *Take a look at Asian Americans you know well. Do you see any Moseses or Aarons? What can we do to develop these rare leader types? Do we need a unique leadership track for budding Moseses?*

Reading about Moses also raises questions for me about the Asian American community:

- *Are there specific things within Asian Americans that keep us from responding to leadership opportunities and challenges? Are there aspects of our culture and heritage that are roadblocks? How might we deal with them?*

- *Why is it we rarely see Asian Americans at the front of the pack when it comes to taking on really big challenges?*

- *Do Asian Americans take on the really big challenges more readily if it is in the context of our own culture? Or when it is set in the arena of the dominant culture?*

had eliminated an entire generation of men, knowing what that would do to a people not given to "marrying out." This must have produced in Moses anger, bitterness and contempt. How do you live under the same roof with the destroyer of your own people?

You don't, if you have a conscience and courage. Moses flees the country, leaving behind his birth family and over thirty-five years of Egyptian upbringing. Taking a water break in Midian, his sense of righteousness protects seven sisters from shepherd thugs and he is rewarded with dinner with the family.

Scripture gives us an abridged version of the next forty years of Moses' life (summarized in seven verses) but we are told this much: he enters an interracial, interreligious marriage with one of the sisters, becomes a shepherd and has a son he names Gershom. Name translation: "I have become an alien in a foreign land."

The plunge into assimilation continues as he forgoes Hebrew tradition by not circumcising his son (Ex 4:24-26). Ironically, it is his non-Hebrew wife Zipporah who takes things into her own hands quite literally to compensate for Moses' denial of his ethnicity.

This is often the case in interracial marriages; the spouse from the majority culture takes the initiative in freeing the partner to own and affirm his or her own ethnicity. When our son entered preschool, it was Deep South Margaret, not Sansei Paul, who approached Sam's teacher to ask if she could come teach a unit on Japanese culture so that Sam could feel proud about his Japanese heritage.

God asks Moses, now eighty, to deliver the Israelites out from under Pharaoh's oppressive thumb. What follows is an almost comical, fairly Asian-sounding "Why me? I'm not worthy" argument between Yahweh and Moses. He raises objections we have heard in our circles or raised ourselves: "I'm unfit for the job." "Why would these people follow *me*?" "Why not someone else?" "I don't speak very well."

This last objection shows Moses' desperation. Acts 7:22 states it plainly: "Moses was educated in all the wisdom of the Egyptians and was *powerful in speech and action*." We identify with Moses feeling overwhelmed by the immensity of the task. We see the cost of this call on his extended family and cringe when he's asked to put God before family.

One senses some pretty decent material here for a movie script. Who can blame Moses? His résumé at age eighty doesn't read like Norman Schwarzkopf's pre-Desert Storm résumé. This is not a virile Charlton Heston at thirty-three here, his age when he played Moses in *The Ten Commandments*. It's more like Heston in 2003 at eighty, the age of Moses the deliverer, long retired and living off his Hollywood pension.

What follows in the rest of the Pentateuch is the amazing account of the development of a leader, one selected by God to change human history. Moses' maturation as a leader is heartening to us who could never believe God could use us to lead others well.

ESTHER

The book of Esther could easily have been written in the early twenty-first century. This amazing account, written nearly 2,500 years ago, tells the story of how God used two unlikely cousins to save their community in exile from extermination at the hands of a volatile despot.

Ethnic cleansing is not a modern phenomena. Those who don't talk, eat, worship, dress and think like the majority culture have always posed a threat to their standards. Fear or hatred of a people because of their skin tone, religious or cultural practices can result into irrational acts of violence. Don't like 'em? Purge 'em.

Xerxes was king of the vast Persian empire which extended from northwest India, across the Near East, into northern Africa and eastern Europe. He reigned from 486 to 465 B.C. He was a quixotic, mercurial leader. What he wanted he usually got. When he didn't, everybody best step back.

One day, around 479 B.C., he beckoned Queen Vashti to a lavish bash he was throwing. It had been going strong for a week and liquor was flowing freely. Persians typically made decisions while drunk then validated them when sober. Xerxes "in high spirits from wine" (Esther 1:10) wanted to show off his beautiful queen. Vashti, however, was having her own "girls' night out" and ignored the king's humiliating invitation. Xerxes' male testosterone went into overdrive. He dethroned her and sent her off to his farm team, his harem.

A search committee was formed and a nationwide search for a suitable replacement was undertaken. When all the votes were in, Esther the Jew won and was crowned as queen. Her older cousin, Mordecai, had been her legal guardian since both her parents died. Mordecai was street savvy; he forbade Esther to let Xerxes know she was a Jew.

When Xerxes appointed Haman to be his right hand, Mordecai refused to bend his knee before Haman, who with his own substantial portion of testosterone becomes furious. Haman decides not to kill only Mordecai, but upon discovering his racial heritage, he decrees on the day before Passover the complete annihilation of Mordecai's people, the Jews. It was ethnic cleansing, pure and simple. Xerxes frees up the funding (more than $5.6 million in today's currency) and blesses Haman's mission.

Mordecai urges Esther to approach the king to reverse his edict. To do so, explains Esther, could result in her death. He comes back with his now famous response:

ESTHER WAS

- an orphan, raised by a relative

- embarrassed by her culture

- challenged to be a "stick-out nail" leader

- faced with ethnic cleansing as a despised minority

- a female leader dealing with testosterone-driven male leaders

- using natural gifting for strategic advantage

- reliant on her cousin Mordecai, who was a strategic planner, had integrity, compassionate for own people, family loyalty

> Do not think that because you are in the king's house you alone of all the Jews will escape. For if you remain silent at this time, relief and deliverance for the Jews will arise from another place, but you and your father's family will perish. *And who knows but that you have come to royal position for such a time as this?* (Esther 4:13-14)

Esther comes to her senses. She utilizes her position as queen to persuade Xerxes to let the Jews live. He agrees and even replaces Haman with Mordecai. Haman who had built gallows to hang Mordecai ends up being hanged on them.

LESSONS FROM ESTHER

Queen Esther overcame huge odds to change human history. Why is this episode a good word for Asian Americans? Four reasons come to mind.

First, she was an orphan, raised by her older cousin. Many Southeast Asian Americans who went through genocidal persecution or wars have been raised without a mother, father or both. Like Esther, they came to a foreign land at an early age and were forced to assimilate.

In 1975 the United States withdrew its forces from all of Southeast Asia. Several hundred thousand Hmong, fearing revenge from the victorious Communist governments of Vietnam and Laos, fled to Thailand where they crowded into crude refugee camps. Between 1975 and 1994, more than 110,000 Hmong refugees resettled in the United States, leaving almost two hundred years of history back in Southeast Asia.

I think of Cambodians who suffered under the radical Khmer Rouge movement from 1975 to 1979. Under leader Pol Pot's totalitarian regime about 1.7 million Cambodians, over one-fifth of the population, were killed and Cambodia fell into economic ruin. More than half a million sought asylum in neighboring Thailand in the 1980s, with over 300,000 eventually resettling in other countries, including the United States.

I also think of children raised by immigrant parents who both work twelve to sixteen hours a day. They sacrifice to give their children a better life than theirs but in the process have little time and energy to parent them well. While not formally orphans, experientially these children often feel abandoned.

Second, though deeply assimilated, she was still a Jew. Esther's people had been exiled from Israel to a land far east 120 years prior to her becoming queen. She was most likely a fourth generation "Jewish Persian." Her ethnic identity crisis hit its apex when cousin Mordecai embarrasses her by donning sackcloth and ashes, going "into the city, wailing loudly and bitterly" when Haman engineers the Jewish holocaust (Esther 4:1). Mordecai calls on Esther "to go into the king's presence to beg for mercy and plead with him for *her* people."

Queen Esther is caught in the same tug-of-war all ethnic minorities find themselves in as they walk the wobbly tightrope of fitting into the larger society and yet not giving up their ethnicity and culture. If she refuses Mordecai's request, she is denying being Jewish. If she accedes to him, she risks her own life. To this point, she has hidden her ethnicity from Xerxes. What looks like a no-brainer from the peanut gallery of the future is much more complex.

Third, Esther's natural beauty put her in contention to replace the deposed Queen Vashti. To put it in the vernacular, Esther was a knockout. She did nothing to make that happen; it came from her Creator's artistry. Similarly Asian Americans have been endowed with natural gifting or prowess that God gave for a purpose. It may be in math, science, medicine, technology or music. It may be something altogether different. Whatever God gives us is meant to be shared for the good of the kingdom in particular and humankind in general.

Fourth, it is cousin Mordecai who provides Esther her ethnic wake-up call. Unlike Esther, whose perspective is clouded, Mordecai is quite clear on who his people are. When he dons sackcloth and ashes, Esther is embarrassed and sends an alternative wardrobe. Mordecai refuses the threads that would allow him to fit into Persian culture and nails his cousin with Esther 4:13-14.

When she does "get it," she clearly understands the risk if she chooses to act. Her years under Mordecai's care and tutelage have driven his values deep into her being. After her initial embarrassment, she throws her lot with her fellow Jews.

For many Asian Americans, it is more convenient to bury or ignore our ethnicity. During my adolescence, teen years and early twenties, the name of the game for Japanese Americans was fit in, don't stick out, and frankly, be as white as possible. My parents' experience behind barbed wire instructed them to assimilate well and as quickly as possible. They knew what being the wrong nationality cost them and no way were they going to have their children pay again. That meant American first names, cars from Detroit and all the activities of my white counterparts. My interpretation, when I tried to make sense of it, was that on a scale of one to ten, white people were tens. Trying my darnedest, the most I could be as a Japanese American was about a seven.

In middle school, I was terribly embarrassed that my hair wasn't blond and my eyes blue. Short of bleaching, I did all I could to blend in and not be different. When it was time to take one of those standardized tests during eighth grade, I found one more way to blend in. I wrote in the name space: Paul Michael Tokunaga. This did wonders for my self-identity until the results came back. Mom sat me down to write five hundred times in longhand: "My name is Paul Minoru Tokunaga." It had been bad enough my last name was Tokunaga, not Thompson or even Token, but to have a foreign middle name was more than my adolescent psyche could handle.

TURNING JAPANESE

I hated being Japanese. Why couldn't I have blond hair? Why couldn't my nose be longer instead of "squashed"? Why couldn't I be "six foot two with eyes of blue" as one popular song went?

In college, something happened that rocked my "white" world to its core. I had a white girlfriend and the relationship was getting serious. After one break, she returned from home and sat me down.

"Paul, we have to break up," she said. "Mom told me I can't date someone who's not white. She asked, 'What will the neighbors say? What will your children look like?' I'm sorry . . ."

Our breakup catalyzed an internal volcanic eruption that yanked my assimilation cord. It was like someone whacked me on the side of the head with a brick. It became crystal clear: I wasn't white, I was never going to be white, and why in the world would I want to be white?

My ethnic awakening took off like a rocket. I began to "own" my Japanese American heritage. The internment experience was still too raw and fresh for my parents to talk about it with their children. *Nisei*, Bill Hosokawa's landmark book about second-generation Japanese Americans, helped me to discover what they and my relatives went through. My pride and respect for them grew immensely. I saw that assimilation was a survival tactic, not just something to gain popularity and friends. Their suffering became my *raison d'être*, my reason for being.

Growing in my ethnic identity, however, was not always a pretty thing. When a pendulum swings, it usually moves from one extreme to the other.

Reverse racism kicked in and I started hating all things white. I sold my VW—made by white folk—and bought a Toyota. I quit wearing Adidas—another "white product"—and only wore Onitsuka Tigers. I began speaking at high schools and social groups about the racism behind the internment of my people. I didn't even try to hide my anger and bitterness.

In retrospect, I'm sure living with me was not always enjoyable for my three white roommates. When I asked one of them to take my picture—dressed up as a kamikaze pilot—in front of a poster in my room of a kamikaze pilot, the Japanese flag, and the words, "Fly the friendly skies," I'm sure he thought I had gone off the deep end. I *had* gone off the deep end, but in time the pendulum swung back into healthier territory.

Owning my Japanese-ness helped me to identify with other minorities, especially Mexican Americans, the largest minority group in San Jose at the time. I struggled to overcome my own childhood prejudices of them as undereducated, poor and having heavy accents my friends and I often ridiculed. When I graduated from college, I soon became involved in fighting for the rights of Mexican migrant farmers in California through the work of Cesar Chavez and the United Farm Workers.

Mom and I would often have long talks into the evening when I would visit them for a few days. Once I mentioned, "I'm proud to be Japanese." She nearly fell off her chair. "You're kidding! I always thought you were ashamed of your Japanese heritage."

"I was ashamed, Mom, but the more I learn what you and Dad went through for our sake, the prouder I get."

Most of us will experience ethnic wake-up calls like Esther's at some point in our lives. For some, it will happen in a moment. For others, the journey can take years. My journey from seeing Japanese Americans as sevens who could actually become tens took about fifteen years of gradual movement, from around age twenty to thirty-five. I'm glad I made the pilgrimage but the road was full of potholes and surprising twists and turns. Each person's journey is uniquely their own. There is no one true roadmap that works for all.

WHAT TO DO ONCE YOU WAKE UP

Mordecai's wake-up call brings to life for Esther his values of family loyalty, compassion for the Jewish community, doing the right thing at all costs and strategic planning. Esther's comfort zone had gotten awfully cushy. To act would risk losing incredible prestige, luxury and privilege. To say "Those are my people" would put her life in mortal danger. Many Asian Americans share that comfort zone. Our parents and their parents have worked hard. We've worked hard. Many of us have a lot. Our toys mean more to us than we care to admit.

As we engage the majority culture, be it at the workplace or in the church, the higher we rise in leadership the more difficult it is to keep a strong ethnic identity. There is subtle pressure to blend in and conform to the high level corporate culture, to become "one of them." It becomes harder to say, "I'm a Japanese American" and easier to just be "an American." We become very conscious of glass ceilings, seeing how being different thickens the ceiling and makes it harder to break through. But perhaps we too have come to a "royal position" for such a time as this.

Street-smart Mordecai gives us insights into how we can be strategic about our ethnic identity. At first he encourages Esther to assimilate completely and not reveal her ethnicity. When she becomes queen and the Jews are on the verge of annihilation, he challenges her to stand up for her people and use her position to stop the violence.

Most of us will be in positions and places where we will be in the minority. Like Esther, we will have times to blend in and then times when we need to stand up for "our people."

Several years ago I was appointed InterVarsity's regional director for the Southeast and attended my first national regional directors meeting. InterVarsity had been in existence for forty-nine years at that time and I was their first nonwhite regional director. Yikes!

Our president was Tom Dunkerton, a former New York-based executive with one of the largest advertising agencies in the world. Tom was very verbal and led freewheeling, open meetings.

For several days I sat and listened, saying very little, taking it all in. Finally, as we discussed ministry to ethnic minority students, I raised my hand. This was a nonhand-raising group but I wasn't comfortable just cutting in. After rehearsing under my breath, I quietly said with trepidation, "Umm . . . I think this is God's special hour for Asian Americans. I, uh, think we should given Asian Americans priority in our campus ministry."

Tom shot up and nearly shouted, "Let's do it!" He then led us in a strategy session of how that might happen. At that time, 22 Asian Americans were on staff, and InterVarsity was working with 1,600 Asian American students. Fourteen years later, we have 105 Asian American campus staff and are working with over 4,000 Asian American students.

ESTHER IN MONTGOMERY, ALABAMA

In 1955, Rosa Parks was a forty-year-old seamstress. In 1945, she tried to board a bus from the front of the bus instead of the back. For ten more years, Mrs. Parks thought about what seat was rightly hers to sit in as a citizen of the U.S. She thought about it for ten years. Twice a day, five days a week for ten years. She thought about it 5,280 times.

By December 1, 1955, she had thought about it 5,281 times. Through her mind: "Uh-uh. No. Can't do. Won't do. They'll have to carry me off to jail and fine me for taking away what's mine."

In 1965, Cleveland Avenue—the bus line she was on when she refused to get up—was renamed Rosa Parks Boulevard. In 1970, Rosa Parks was awarded the NAACP's highest honor, the Spingarn Medal. In 1980, she was given the prestigious Martin Luther King, Jr. Award. In 1987 she founded the Rosa and Raymond Parks Institute for Self Development, which provides scholarships and guidance for young blacks. In 1996 President Bill Clinton awarded her the Presidential Medal of Freedom, the highest honor that the U.S. government can give to a civilian.

When I think of Rosa Parks, I think civil rights giant, courageous crusader, a lay-down-your-lifer. She's a legend and rightly so. She's right up there with Martin Luther King when I think of Hall of Fame-type heroes.

But here's what we need to remember about Rosa Parks. *She was a seamstress.* Her husband was a barber. She wasn't a preacher. She led an ordinary, quiet life. A background check shows an activity just months before that helped prepare her for this situation; she had gone to a "summer leadership camp" on civil disobedience tactics. She trained for this.

Had she just gotten up out of her seat when the bus driver told her to get up, she would have continued on in her ordinary life. Cleveland Avenue in Montgomery would still be Cleveland Avenue. Rosa Parks was an ordinary person who stepped up.

What do *you* see when you look into the mirror each morning? Do you see Rosa Parks? Do you see an ordinary person?

Will you step up?

ASIAN AMERICAN ROSA PARKS: FOR SUCH A TIME AS THIS

As Asian Americans, it is deeply embedded in us *not* to step up. If anything, we are trained to step *down*. What happens to the nail that sticks out? It should be hammered down. We aren't supposed to stand out, make a fuss or draw attention to ourselves. Defer, let others go first, give up your seat. This may be cultural, but it is not necessarily godly.

Our God is a more than a little crazy. He loves to take seamstresses and have them sew a tapestry like no one could ever imagine.

Are you a Rosa Parks? Are you ordinary? Are you the nail that is *always ready to be hammered down?* If you are, *stop it.* Stop being hammered down. Stop refusing to step up. Quit stepping down.

Esther was told by Mordecai, "For perhaps you have been called to royal dignity for such a time as this." Is this your time? Are you an Asian American Rosa Parks? What is the bus that God has placed in your life?

Marian Wright Edelman writes in *Lanterns: A Memoir to Mentors,* "Mrs. Parks was just the right person at the right time to light the spark that light the movement that Montgomery NAACP head E. B. Nixon had been vigilantly working, watching, and waiting for. He had a plan and an infrastructure ready to go when the right case and opportunity arose."

She continues, "God chooses the actors, the times, the places, sets the stage, lifts the curtain and begins the drama. Our task is to be ready to play our parts and to do the work God assigns us without anxiety according to the strengths and gifts we are given."[2]

QUESTIONS FOR US FROM ESTHER'S LIFE

- Do you have a Mordecai, someone who can shoot straight with you

about both where your life is missing the mark and what it can become?

- If you have a Mordecai, are you giving them access to your secrets—
  ambitions, sins, struggles, temptations?

- If you don't have a Mordecai, ask God to bring one to you. Pray with
  faith and be open to whom God might bring your way. Don't come with
  a shopping list; his Mordecai for you may be a surprise. It may not be
  an Asian American.

- Esther was blessed with beauty. What natural giftings has God given
  you that can used by him to help others?

- Like Esther becoming queen, have you been offered a platform for influencing? Have you accepted or declined it? If you accepted it, were
  you able to influence and lead well? If you declined it, what were your
  reasons? Were they valid reasons or were you copping out?

- Esther is a fourth or fifth generation "Jewish Persian" who has assimilated well into Persian culture. Her ethnicity doesn't stand out nor does
  it inform much of her self-identity. As an Asian American, do you
  "own" your ethnicity? Is it something of which you are proud, ashamed
  or maybe in denial of?

- Mordecai pops the big question to Esther, "And who knows but that
  you have come to royal position for such a time as this?" Have you ever
  been in a situation where you sensed this, not as a queen but as one
  placed in a position of potential influence? How did you handle it?

- Do you see yourself as a "Rosa Parks, seamstress"—someone ordinary?
  Are you willing to "step up" like Mrs. Parks did? Put another way, are
  you willing to be the nail that sticks out and *not* be nailed down?

BECOMING A REALLY GOOD LEADER

Keep Doing Five Things; Quit Doing Three Others

Famous lines never said by an Asian American:

"I am the greatest!" (Muhammad Ali)

"I am the greatest star!" (Barbra Streisand in *Funny Girl*)

"I will be in the All-Star Game in two years." (Josh Beckett, 19, at his contract signing; two years later, at the time of the 2001 All-Star game, Beckett was seen pitching for the Florida Marlins AA farm team)

"I'm the king of the world!" (Leonardo DiCaprio in *Titanic*)

"You . . . like . . . me, . . . you . . . really . . . like . . . me!" (Sally Field's acceptance speech for winning an Academy Award in 1979 for *Norma Rae*)

"May God have mercy upon my enemies, because I won't." (General George Patton)

T-shirts never worn by an Asian American:

"If all the world is a stage, I want better lighting."

"People who think they know it all are especially annoying to those of us who do."

"We'll get along fine as soon as you realize I'm God."

What Asian Americans aren't good at is admitting what we are good at. Indulge me to take you outside the box for a few minutes. It won't hurt too much and like medicine, it will be good for you.

YOU GET THINGS DONE, NOTICED BY OTHERS OR NOT

"You can count on me" could be your anthem. Asian Americans tend to be the "go to" people when things need to get done. You are *omoiyari* people who "seek to optimize each other's comfort by seeking to provide

pleasure or prevent displeasure by anticipating the other's needs and desires and taking initiative to meet those needs and fulfill them without the
other person having to overtly express them in some obvious way."[1]

Omoiyari people are very communal and loyal by nature. For any
community to function well, it needs some members who see the
needs and then figure out how to meet them. Receiving recognition is
nice but not the driving force for *omoiyari* people. Being the oil between gears doesn't get headlines but the machine comes to a jarring
stop without it.

Japanese American June was missions coordinator for our predominantly white fellowship at Florida State. During leadership team meetings, her soft voice was rarely heard above the din created by the eight
other leaders. She couldn't compete in volume and would never consider
cutting off another's comments to express her opinion. Only when Roger,
the president, said, "What are you thinking, June?" would they quiet
down enough to give June a little air time.

At year's end, when evaluating our ministry on campus, June's impact
was clearly felt. She had directed the first-ever student missions conference for north Florida colleges. Even more impressive was that *every*
member of the all-student leadership team was planning on going on a
summer missions trip or exploring a career in missions. Roger sensed
God's call to church planting in Latin America. Beth was doing a summer
missions project in Alabama. Clark was praying about serving in West Africa. Betsy was exploring options with Wycliffe Bible Translators. The
others on the team—John, Darlene, J. P. and Linda, along with June, were
all exploring missions opportunities.

Quietly but effectively she had personally encouraged each of them to
explore their role in global missions. When I discovered this, I told her
what an incredible job she had done.

"Oh no, Paul," she said. "I didn't do anything. It was the Holy Spirit
working in their lives."

"That's right, June. But it was *you* the Holy Spirit worked through to
elevate missions in the fellowship."

After a few more rounds of "oh, no" and "oh, yes," I conceded in convincing June how much God had used her to make missions a frontburner issue in the fellowship.

YOU BUILD COHESIVE, INTERDEPENDENT NUCLEAR FAMILIES

For all of the talk of conflicts in Asian American families, the good news is your families are intact enough to make such difficulties possible. Many of your non-Asian counterparts can't relate to your family issues. Family? What family?

Your families are there for you. Most of you haven't had to think twice about the essentials: decent housing, family meals, transportation, savings for college. Your parents poured themselves into providing those things, rarely with complaint.

They have put family first and have asked you to do the same. The result has generally been an anomaly in American society: long marriages, growing up at a slower rate than your non-Asian peers, deep commitment between siblings, children often being their parents' retirement plan.

I visited a Chinese American student who was in her senior year and aiming for med school. I asked if she would return to her hometown to set up her practice. "Maybe, but probably not," she said. I knew she was tight with her family.

"How would that be for your folks if you didn't return?"

"Oh, that wouldn't be a problem. They'd move to wherever I end up." I wasn't sure I had heard her correctly so I asked her to repeat it.

"They would do that?"

"Oh, yeah."

"You would want that?"

Thoughtful pause. "Oh, yeah."

Your family upbringing—warts, weaknesses and all—can be a gift to those who come from families less endowed. Though I was hypercritical of my own family as a teenager and young adult, spending time in my friends' homes fleshed out the range of possibilities of what a family could be like.

Mark Twain nailed it when he said, "When I was a boy of fourteen, my father was so ignorant I could hardly stand to have the old man around.

But when I got to be twenty-one, I was astonished at how much the old man had learned in seven years." In retrospect, my family provided more for me than my limited vision could take in but Planet Paul couldn't see it at the time.

As you lead others, part of your mentoring and developing plan might be including them for meals, visits and vacations with your own family. Nobody does the nonblood related, extended family thing like Asian Americans. Within your family, are there potential "aunties and uncles" who could provide warmth, wisdom and a knockout meal for your friends? Could *you* be someone's auntie or uncle?

YOU HONOR YOUR ELDERS

The honoring doesn't stop with your parents. Gray hair is good, on your parents or others. American Association of Retired Persons membership is esteemed not hidden. Wednesday grocery shopping with the five percent senior discount rocks. Confucius gets a lot of the kudos for engineering Asian elder-honoring.

As I cross the half-century line, I'm liking this. Working with young Asian Americans has its upside. I always get a thank you card when I speak at an Asian American meeting, usually signed by most of the group. They wouldn't think of asking me to room with them twenty-to-a-bathroom at a conference. And I never, *ever* go hungry.

By not dismissing your elders, you are privy to wisdom only distilled by years of experience. In the context of church, such honoring creates a strong bond that knits generations together. How might you "market your elders" even better?

In the church, having the pastor "bless" elders and younger adults spending time together helps create an open atmosphere. From there, initiative can be taken on both ends: young adults could approach certain elders they would like to meet with and elders could ask young adults out for breakfast before church. Asking for help and offering help is often a tad awkward. Am I being too forward? What if they say no, do I lose face with them? But when cross-generational mentoring happens, the payoffs can be enormous for both receiver and giver.

SUPERVISING AN ELDER

What happens when a younger person is asked to supervise or oversee someone older? There are no guarantees but the following scenarios might reveal some possible outcomes and what each party could do.

1. *Both are Asian American: awkward for both. I would encourage the younger supervisor to address the issue head-on. Ask, "Are you comfortable being supervised by someone younger?" Voice your own awkwardness of supervising an elder. Though it may feel threatening, ask for their counsel in situations where their experiences can be drawn upon. Look for ways to honor their years of service.*

   For the elder, affirm that the sovereign God ultimately places people where he thinks will be best. Pray for humility and a submissive spirit. Look for ways to help your supervisor succeed. Let your legacy be that you helped a young leader with potential come into their own.

2. *Supervisor is Asian American and younger than non-Asian American supervised: awkward for the supervisor, not necessarily awkward for the person supervised.*

   When I had been that younger supervisor, I kept telling myself, "This is probably more awkward for me than for them." I worked hard at being more of a servant than a lord. When I felt secure enough in my own leadership, I would look for

ways to promote their success in the organization. If it is someone who wanted your position, awkwardness is inevitable. You will be scrutinized and judged, perhaps unfairly. It's fair to ask your own supervisor to help make this potentially delicate relationship work.

   You may hear second-hand, "Paul got the job because he's a minority." How to respond? "Thank you. I hope my perspective and uniqueness as a minority leader will strengthen and better this organization." Debating the claim is an emotional drainer with no winners.

3. *Supervisor is not Asian American and younger than the Asian American supervised: not necessarily awkward for the supervisor, possibly very awkward for the person supervised. Whites and others from nonhierarchal cultures are often used to having younger bosses or supervising others older than them. You are likely to feel more awkward than your younger, non-Asian American supervisor. Try to clue them in on this dynamic and how it affects you.*

   If you desired your supervisor's position, your difficulty will likely be compounded. Give them grace to not do things perfectly or as you might. In the end, it may be an unworkable situation and you may need to be repositioned.

When we started getting involved at Atlanta Chinese Christian Church, I was struck and impressed by the mentoring and accountability relationships in the English congregation. Young adults were mentoring those in the youth group. Youth group members were in accountability groups. Because such relationships were part of the church's DNA, Patrick and James didn't hesitate to ask me if I would mentor them. The blessings flow both ways. These two relationships have been the highlight of my involvement at ACCC.

Honoring one's elders seems to be characteristic of many ethnic minority groups, not just Asian Americans. American culture, on the other hand, encourages familiarity and casualness. Age differences and generation gaps are meant to be bridged.

Recently I spent time with a Caucasian family that I have known for decades. The sixteen-year old son shouted affectionately at me, "Shut up, P. Daddy!" (Not to be confused with rapper P. Diddy!) He felt comfortable with me and was reaching out to me with his new nickname for me. After the shock wore off, it made me feel good and a part of the family. I also knew I would never be called P. Daddy by Asian American high schoolers.

YOU PUT A HIGH VALUE ON CHURCH INVOLVEMENT

For those who grew up in Asian American churches, church means extended family. A church where one has grown up with twenty "aunties" and "uncles"—none blood-related—provides a safety net of secure relationships.

When you relocate to a new city, expectations for a church run high. An hour on Sunday, maybe two counting Sunday school, does not constitute church for you. Good preaching, often the benchmark of an acceptable church home for most non-Asian Americans, is not enough. It has to feel like family.

You're not content to be consumers only. You're willing and eager to pitch in to serve and lead. If you happen to leave one church for another, it's usually due not to burnout but often to being underutilized. You want to be players.

For those who have been active in campus fellowships the ante is even higher. On campus, you've led Bible studies, served on worship teams, done strategic planning, discipled younger students, shared your faith, given talks, served on a summer missions trip or urban project, coordinated daily prayer meetings. You've tasted ministry firsthand and it tasted good.

Many of you are quite competent in several of these areas and could step in immediately and contribute. Others need a bit more seasoning and help in translating their campus experiences to the church. Nothing is more frustrating than to be told to wait your turn . . . and wait . . . and wait. It's especially hard when things you do well are done poorly.

Timothy Tseng, associate professor of American religious history at American Baptist Seminary of the West, says, "Unless first-generation leaders are able to give second-generation pastors [leaders] the freedom to lead, their young people will not go to these churches. First-generation pastors need to be aware of this dynamic."[2]

A few words of advice from the University of Been There and Messed Up:

- Pray for grace and the ability to view the church from the leaders' perspective, not just your own.

- Don't try to transform the church into your campus fellowship; they're two different organisms and were meant to be.

- Pray for humility and be willing to take on tasks below your level of expertise.

- Pour yourself into one or two other church members; their spiritual growth will help you cope with the structure that doesn't change as quickly as you would like.

YOU GATHER PEOPLE AND GAIN CONSENSUS

Asian Americans are "groupies." Not of the rock star backstage variety, but of the "we don't go solo" sort. You are strongly communal, which means you both support and depend on others. That's healthy and biblical:

> *Two are better than one,*
> *because they have a good return for their work:*
> *If one falls down,*
> *his friend can help him up.*

> *But pity the man who falls*
> *and has no one to help him up!* (Eccles 4:9-10)

You are good at bringing people together, particularly fellow Asian Americans. You tend to like meetings of most any type because it means you can be with people you enjoy. Companionship overrides any agenda.

You are also good at arriving at consensus when decisions are to be made. Everyone's opinion matters. While the group might not be able to come to complete agreement, it would feel fundamentally wrong for the leader to decide without hearing everyone out. The upside is obvious—few feel ignored.

You may take being a gatherer for granted. Doesn't everybody do this?

Nope. Especially in churches and fellowships low in Asian Americans, bringing people together may not happen as naturally as you are used to. If it's a multiethnic church or fellowship, there will naturally be insiders and outsiders. It's our nature. You bring something special and necessary. My advice is simple—gather on!

The downside of needing one hundred percent agreement is that it can take forever and a day to make mundane decisions. You may also lose some folks (read: non-Asian Americans) who have grown up with "majority rules" and go nuts waiting for everyone to agree.

My advice is to work for as much consensus as possible in a reasonable amount of time. Having all onboard is nice but usually not necessary to move forward with plans. Leading well means saying, "That's good input, folks. Here's what we are going to do."

But before we call ourselves God's gift to the world, consider the flip side. We need to quit doing three things. Some habits are awfully hard to break. Many are lifelong patterns. We can't expect them to go away overnight. They also won't disappear by our sheer individual willpower. We need the help of the Holy Spirit and our Christian community. Here are three patterns that need to stop.

QUIT KEEPING OUR TREASURES TO OURSELVES

The flip side of one of our strengths reveals a gaping weakness. While we create strong communal ties, we tend to keep the family treasures to ourselves. We have much to offer but we hoard it. Such selfishness might be leading Asian Americans down a road to disaster.

In May 2001, the Committee of 100, an organization that addresses issues concerning Chinese Americans, released a comprehensive report, "American Attitudes Towards Chinese Americans and Asian Americans." Researchers conducted ten focus groups—two comprising Asian Americans and eight comprising non-Asian Americans. Four groups were held in New York, four in Los Angeles and two in Chicago.

One of their findings was encouraging: "The non-Asian Americans polled had a high regard for the hard work, family focus, ambition, commitment to education and the intellectual gifts of Asian Americans." Interpretation: we have a lot to offer others.

Then came the bad news: The most frequently mentioned criticism of Asian Americans: "They stick together" and "They are cliquish/clannish." The non-Asian Americans saw Asian Americans as being less likely to be full participants in the entire community as other Americans. They were seen to be more inward looking. Many non-Asian Americans described Asian Americans as arrogant, aloof, keeping to themselves, disinterested in and disapproving of the larger American community and not approachable. These were reactions to the perceived success of Asian Americans. (See chapter eleven for other findings of the survey.) Attitudes like these come from perceptions, some fraught with stereotypes, others justified and accurate. How do we change how we are seen? For starters, we need to "unclump."

A ghetto is by definition "any section of a city which many members of some minority groups live, or to which they are restricted as by economic pressure or social discrimination." Asian Americans are often guilty as charged of living in a cultural ghetto. As Pastor Soong-Chan Rah of Cambridge Community Fellowship Church aptly puts it, Asian Americans are "clumpers."

On campus we clump together like we're wearing magnets. Where to find us? Together in the dining hall. Together in our own social clubs. Together at the bowling alley, movie theater or restaurant. Forever together.

Our churches combine as our place of worship and our social center.

They are our primary clump centers. We clump by nationality and then we clump further by language and once more by dexterity with that language. While there is great value in having friendships with Asian Americans, having only Asian American friends is unhealthy. Our worlds stay small, our crosscultural skills stagnate and we deprive others of the joy of knowing us.

Such isolationism causes those unlike us to form stereotypes to describe us. Is it fair on our part to lash out or scream "Foul!" when we get negatively stereotyped when we are not willing to develop friendships with those not Asian American?

> **TWO QUESTIONS TO CONSIDER:**
>
> - *Of my five closest friends, how many are not Asian American?*
>
> - *Who are three non-Asian Americans with whom I might step up my involvement, sharing God's good gifts to me with them?*

When was the last time you and an African American, Hispanic American or Caucasian American

- ate a meal at your place?
- visited your family's home for the weekend?
- went on a date?
- went to your Asian American church together, if you attend one?

When all our friendships are with those just like us, it robs the gospel of authenticity and power. It implies, "My God is for me and my friends like me. He's not for you." It makes him into a tribal deity, not the God for all people.

Unclumping only happens when we intentionally do it. It's hard to make changes, but it's worth it. In a chapter titled "Gifts Asian Americans Bring" in *Following Jesus Without Dishonoring Your Parents*, I discuss five gifts or qualities Asian Americans often have that need to be shared with others: deep friendship and community identity, hospitality evangelism, being bridge people for racial healing, our wealth and education, and the gift of pain. We have stuff needed by others.

The apostle Paul put it like this: "If the whole body were an eye, where would the sense of hearing be? If the whole body were an ear, where would the sense of smell be? God has arranged the parts in the body, every one of them just as he wanted them to be" (1 Cor 12:17-18). The body of Christ—non-Asian Americans included—needs what we have to bring.

QUIT FAILING SO POORLY

William Faulkner expresses it well: "It's hard believing but disaster seems to be good for people." Success in leadership gives us the gumption to keep moving forward, open to new horizons. Failure forces us to step back, catch our breath and wonder if we were cut out for leading. *Failing is good for us and it makes us better leaders—as long as we don't quit.*

I tend not to learn much from my successes because I have high expectations for myself. I climb a mountain, I look up for the next one. Success for me derails healthy reflection.

As Asian Americans, we are particularly good at not failing well. Perhaps because our family set the bar so high we are driven toward perfectionism. Others of us don't have to blame our parents; we are perfectionistic enough on our own, thank you very much. Bs for us are like Ds for most others. Getting into a second rung graduate school is unthinkable. Feeling confused about a "good Asian career" choice is downright scary.

Being of a shame-based culture also exacerbates failure. I haven't just let down another person or a few, I have disappointed or disgraced *my people.*

Here's the irony: failing is liberating after we get over the horror of doing it. When I fail, I pull out the full-length mirror and gaze long and hard. On my good post-failure days, I ask questions like

What did I do well? I don't let myself move on until I've been fair to myself with this question. Often when I fail, I can't believe I did anything right and well. That's usually untrue.

Who did I hurt by my mistakes? Do I need to make amends with anyone? Satan gets real close to me in these moments to tell me I hurt lots of people in lots of ways and I'm unfit to lead again. Taking a reality check with a supervisor or close friend is a good antidote.

The next time I do this task or take on that role, what one or two adjust-

ments can I make so the outcome is different? Chances are an overhaul is not necessary though our perfectionist genes try to convince us otherwise.

On my bad postfailure days, my internal commentary runs something like this: *How could I have done that? What was I thinking? I am such an idiot! Worm! Jerk! No way I'll lead again! So-and-so (any so-and-so!) could have done so much better! How am I going to face those I failed again?*

Recently, I was leading a daylong workshop on multiethnic training for our new area directors. Our last session was a panel I titled "When You Fail." I asked each panel member to talk about one of their personal failures, how they handled it and what they learned from it.

SHAME MEETS GRACE

Games four and five of the 2001 World Series gave us a clear picture of Asian shame at its worst.

Going into the bottom of the ninth in game four, the Arizona Diamondbacks were ahead 3-1 and up two games to one. Diamondbacks manager Bob Brenly turned to his closer, twenty-two year old Korean Byung-Hyun Kim, who then gave up both the game-tying and game-ending homeruns. The series was now tied at two games apiece. Brenly took a beating by the media for lifting ace Curt Schilling for the second-year pitcher from Korea.

In game five, with the Diamondbacks up 2-0 in the eighth, Brenly again brought in Kim. After getting two out, it looked like a smart, gutsy move by Brenly to pick Kim up off the shame heap he was surely languishing on.

Light-hitting Yankee Scott Brosius

promptly hit the first pitch deep into the left field stands. Home run. While Yankee Stadium roared loud enough to wake up Babe Ruth and Lou Gehrig, Kim dropped to a squat behind the pitcher's mound, hands covering his face. The camera close-up seemed to say it all: I am the first Korean-born ever to play in a World Series. I've let down my team, I've let down my family and seventeen generations of Kims, and I've let down my country.

All across America and likely Korea, that picture graced the front page of hundreds of sports sections. I visualized thousands of Asians watching on television like me, emotionally squatting with Kim, covering our faces, sharing his shame.

What happened next was astounding, creating a photo op even better than Kim squatting.

When it was my turn, I said something like this: "My biggest failure is that I don't fail. What I mean is I avoid situations and relationships where the possibility of failing is high. I tend to stay in my comfort zone where I'm less likely to fail."

Sure enough, a few days later, I failed. Isn't that just like God to have such remarkable timing? Since my comments were still fresh, I had to tell God, "You are way too good at this!"

My failure was making a decision that was borderline unethical. It would have been easier to swallow if I had caught myself in the act and altered my actions, but my decision was called into question by my new supervisor,

---

Fourteen-year veteran first baseman Mark Grace was in his first World Series, having just come to Arizona after spending his whole career with the perennially hapless Chicago Cubs. If the Diamondbacks wanted to win this Series for any one player, it would have been for the thirty-seven-year-old Grace. Some people were rooting for the Diamondbacks solely because they felt Grace deserved it for serving a long-term sentence with the Cubbies.

Grace ran over from first base, cradled Kim's head in his arms and held him. We may never find out what he said, but clearly Mark Grace came to extend grace. Most people would have expected him to say, "Kim—you blankety-blank! You took it away from me!" And who could blame him?

After the game, Kim spoke through an interpreter: "I am so sorry to my

teammates and my manager for giving up the tying run. I want to thank my manager for giving me another chance to pitch."

Thanks to incredible comebacks in games six and seven, the Diamondbacks won the series. One of the most memorable scenes of the postgame celebration was Curt Schilling and Byung-Hyun Kim embracing, jumping up and down together—Schilling feeling ecstasy, Kim, enormous relief. After game seven, Kim said, "I'm in heaven. I feel like I'm in heaven."

Perhaps now 68 million Koreans, 1.1 million Korean Americans and all of Arizona could forget his shameful performance in games four and five.

And thank God for Grace. One might even say where shame abounds, there abounds grace even more.

<table>
</table>

FOUR STEPS FOR BEGINNERS AT FAILURE

1. *Choose to do something in which you're not naturally gifted or have had eight years of professional lessons to master it. If it's too much to consider doing alone, find a partner in crime who can fail as successfully as you.*

2. *Adopt friends who love you so much they will search for things in which you can fail grandly. Fight your desire to fight their suggestions.*

3. *Just do it.*

4. *Repeat steps 1 through 3.*

whom I wanted to impress. Though my shame level rose dramatically, failing was good for me. I had to admit my fault and repent. Even forgiveness didn't take away the sting of doing wrong and getting caught.

It was a good wake-up call. It took about a week before my shame level dropped low enough for me to agree with G. K. Chesterton when he said, "I believe in getting into hot water; it keeps you clean."

QUIT DENYING OUR ROLE AS AGENTS OF RACIAL RECONCILIATION

Asian Americans have long carried on outside the battlefield between blacks and whites. Since it's not part of our history, we refuse to claim ownership. We're very content to let it be their issue, their problem. That ought not be an option open to us. At the least, we should see divisions between black and white Christians as our business. If one part of the body suffers, all suffer.

However, before God can use us as agents of reconciliation between blacks and whites, we need to clean up our own house. We need to work toward healthier relationships between Asian nationalities.

Truth be told, most of us carry enough stereotypes and prejudices against other Asians to keep us busy forgiving and reconciling for a good long while. Some of us have the extra weight of history to make peace with.

Taking leadership in inter-Asian racial healing and reconciliation will need people who

- will read honest history to find out the truth about events and relationships between Asian nations.

- like Nehemiah, own the failings of our forbearers, *even generations ago and thousands of miles away.* "I confess the sins we Israelites, including myself and my father's house, have committed against you. We have acted very wickedly toward you. We have not obeyed the commands, decrees and laws you gave your servant Moses." (Neh 1:6-7)

- repent and ask forgiveness for the pain and problems our forebears caused.
- work at restoring healthy relationships with the progeny of those our forbearers abused.

WHAT MIGHT SUCH RECONCILIATION LOOK LIKE?

In 1994 close to five hundred international students representing sixty-eight nations gathered at the University of Illinois. On the second evening of the conference, students met by nationality to pray for their countries. As the contingent from Japan prayed, they asked God if they should repent publicly for the atrocious sins of their nation against other Asian nations. They continued to pray the following day.

That night a Korean student asked if their delegation could join the Japanese in prayer. About fifty students gathered. As the Koreans prayed for the Japanese, they began to weep and confess their hardness of heart for not forgiving Japan. Next the Japanese confessed the sins of their nation. The Koreans sang a blessing song for the Japanese, opening their hands and reaching out to the Japanese as they sang. The Japanese knelt down on the floor with their hands stretched out to receive the blessing.

Setsue Kuroda from Japan reported, "It was as though the transparent wall between us was completely taken away and there was no longer anything to stop us to enjoy and love one another. What a night!"

Kuroda said, "The next morning, in front of the entire conference, the Japanese delegation came forward, knelt and repented for the past and present sins of ourselves and our nation, Japan. Our Korean brothers and sisters returned this act of repentance. I believe the praise songs which they then led and sang for us were the most beautiful noise made before the Lord."

Amazing but true—when we deal with some of our "family issues," God can use us as peacemakers and reconcilers in the broader racial arena, perhaps even between blacks and whites.

BECOMING A GREAT LEADER

Asian American Level 5 Leaders

A recent television commercial makes me both chuckle and wince. In it a klutzy, bespectacled, chubby, balding middle-aged man is walking along a busy downtown street, trips, almost knocks over a woman, then ambles up the steps to a skyscraper. He is the nerd's nerd. The voice-over tells us his story. He failed at several business endeavors. We're clearly convinced this guy is a loser in the first degree. We don't want to identify with him.

As he walks into the building, the camera pans upward to the building's façade. In huge letters, there it is—his name. I laugh because he's laughable. I wince because he reminds me of many Asian Americans. Then I cheer because I believe it can happen.

Jim Collins is the coauthor of *Built to Last: Successful Habits of Visionary Companies,* which was on *BusinessWeek's* bestseller list for sixty-six weeks. In 2001, at the culmination of a massive five-year research project, Collins wrote the aptly titled *Good to Great: Why Some Companies Make the Leap . . . and Others Don't.* From 1996 to 2000, Collins's twenty-two research associates sought to answer one question: "Can a good company become a great company and, if so, how?"

They studied companies that had fifteen years of humble stock market returns punctuated by a transition period, and then fifteen years of returns three times higher than the market between 1965 and 2000. They then identified comparison companies—those in the same industry with the same opportunities and similar resources at the time of transition—that had failed to make that sustained shift. They collected nearly six thousand articles, conducted eighty-seven interviews with key executives, analyzed companies' internal strategy documents, culled through analysts' reports, and much more. The project consumed 10.5 people years of research.

Table 9.1. Good to Great Companies and Their Comparisons

Good-to-Great Companies	Direct Comparisons
Abbott	Upjohn
Circuit City	Silo
Fannie Mae	Great Western
Gillette	Warner-Lambert
Kimberly-Clark	Scott Paper
Kroger	A&P
Nucor	Bethlehem Steel
Philip Morris	R.J. Reynolds
Pitney Bowes	Addressograph
Walgreens	Eckerd's
Wells Fargo	Bank of America

Out of 1,435 companies that have appeared on the Fortune 500 since 1965, only eleven companies qualified as good-to-great (see table 9.1). When the research team looked for repeated themes in these eleven companies, they were surprised with the outcome: a certain combination of qualities were found in *all* of the CEOs in the eleven companies during their fifteen-year transition from being a good company to being transformed into a great one.

Collins described these leaders this way: "The most powerfully transformative executives possess a paradoxical mixture of personal humility and professional will. They are timid and ferocious. Shy and fearless. They are rare—and unstoppable."[1]

COLLINS'S 5 LEVELS OF LEADERSHIP

- *Level 1 Highly Capable Individual: Makes productive contributions through talent, knowledge, skills and good work habits.*

- *Level 2 Contributing Team Member: Contributes to the achievement of group objectives; works effectively with others in a group setting.*

- *Level 3 Competent Manager: Organizes people and resources toward the effective and efficient pursuit of predetermined objectives.*

- *Level 4 Effective Leader: Catalyzes commitment to and vigorous pursuit of a clear and compelling vision; stimulates the group to high performance standards.*

- *Level 5 Executive: [In addition to embodying the qualities in the first four levels,] builds enduring greatness through a paradoxical combination of personal humility plus professional will.[2]*

Collins calls it Level 5 leadership. Coupled with a small handful of other factors, Level 5 leadership was vital in the sustained excellence of these eleven companies.

In the *Harvard Business Review* article, Collins goes on:

> Good-to-great transformations don't happen without Level 5 leaders at the helm. They just don't. Our discovery of Level 5 leadership is counterintuitive. Indeed, it is countercultural. People generally assume that transforming companies from good to great requires larger-than-life leaders—big personalities like [Lee] Iacocca, [Al] Dunlap, [Jack] Welch, and [Stanley] Gault—who make headlines and become celebrities.[3]

DARWIN SMITH: ASIAN AMERICAN ROLE MODEL?

To illustrate, Collins tells the story of Darwin E. Smith, the in-house lawyer of Kimberly-Clark. "A seemingly ordinary man," Smith was named chief executive in 1971 and in twenty years turned it from a "stodgy old paper company" into the "leading consumer paper products company in the world." Under Smith's leadership, one dollar invested in Kimberly-Clark stock in 1971 was worth $39.87 in 1991, outperforming stalwart companies like Hewlett-Packard, 3M, Coca-Cola and General Electric.

Compared with the Iacoccas and Welches, "Darwin Smith seems to have come from Mars. Shy, unpretentious, even awkward, Smith shunned attention. But if you were to consider Smith soft or meek, you would be terribly mistaken. His lack of pretense was coupled with a fierce, even stoic, resolve toward life."[4] Smith was not alone in his anonymity as a CEO.

Despite their remarkable results, almost no one [in the research] remarked about them! George Cain, Alan Wurtzel, David Maxwell, Colman Mockler, Darwin Smith, Jim Herring, Lyle Everingham, Joe Cullman, Fred Allen, Cork Walgreen, Carl Reichardt—how many of these extraordinary executives had you heard of?[5]

The research team was struck by how, in contrast to "the very I-centric style" of the comparison leaders, the good-to-great leaders didn't talk about themselves. Frequently heard comments from Level 5 leaders:

- "I hope I am not sounding like a big shot."

- "If the board hadn't picked such great successors, you probably wouldn't be talking with me today."

- "Did I have a lot to do with it? Oh, that sounds so self-serving. I don't think I can take much credit. We were blessed with marvelous people."

- "There's plenty of people in this company who could do my job better than I do."

They found that people who worked with these select leaders continually described them using words like *"quiet, humble, modest, reserved, shy, gracious, mild-mannered, self-effacing, understated, did not believe his own clippings and so forth."* Collins writes, "The good-to-great leaders never wanted to become larger-than-life heroes. They never aspired to be put on a pedestal or become unreachable icons. They were seemingly ordinary people quietly producing extraordinary results."[6]

And are they very few in number and extremely far-between? Collins doesn't think so. "I believe—although I cannot prove—that potential Level 5 leaders are highly prevalent in our society. *The problem is not, in my estimation, a dearth of potential Level 5 leaders. They exist all around us, if we just know what to look for.* And what is that? Look for situations where extraordinary results exist but where no individual steps forth to claim excess credit. You will likely find a potential Level 5 leader at work."[7]

LEVEL 5 LEADERS: MODEST AND WILLFUL, SHY AND FEARLESS

Level 5 leaders are a study in duality: modest and willful, shy and fearless. Collins draws the contrast in table 9.2.

Table 9.2. Characteristics of Level 5 Leaders

Personal Humility	Professional Will
Demonstrates a compelling modesty, shunning public adulation; never boastful.	Creates superb results, a clear catalyst in the transition from good to great.
Acts with quiet, calm determination; relies principally on inspired standards, not inspiring charisma, to motivate.	Demonstrates an unwavering resolve to do whatever must be done to produce the best long-term results, no matter how difficult.
Channels ambition into the company, not the self; sets up successors for even more greatness in the next generation.	Sets the standard of building an enduring great company; will settle for nothing less.
Looks in the mirror, not out the window, to apportion responsibility for poor results, never blaming other people, eternal factors, or bad luck.	Looks out the window, not in the mirror, to apportion credit for the success of the company—to other people, external factors, and good luck.

To this list Collins adds several more traits of Level 5 leaders: They are ambitious, to be sure, but ambitious first and foremost for the company, not themselves. They set up their successors for even greater success in the next generation, whereas egocentric Level 4 leaders often set up their successors for failure. Level 5 leaders are fanatically driven, infected with an incurable need to produce sustained *results;* they are resolved to do whatever it takes to make the company great, no matter how big or hard the decisions. They display a workmanlike diligence—more plow horse than show horse.

One of the most damaging trends in recent history is the tendency (especially by boards of directors) to select dazzling, celebrity leaders and to deselect potential Level 5 leaders. Ten of the eleven good-to-great CEOs came from *inside* the company, whereas the comparison companies tried outside CEOs six times more often.

You may be scratching your head and mumbling, "Huh? I thought this was a book for Asian American Christian leaders." Or perhaps you're doing somersaults, in your own Darwin Smith kind of way. *You get it.* You made the connection.

We have been told for decades that given our makeup, disposition, gifting—call it what you like—Asian Americans were not CEO, top dog material. They call us good number crunchers or

If Collins's study is on-target, and given its comprehensiveness it seems to be, there's hope the glass ceiling might be shattered for some Asian Americans.

invaluable second-in-command or consummate team players but the hot seat belongs to guys named Iacocca and Welch. And because we look "out the window, not in the mirror, to apportion credit for the success of the company" it isn't our way to nominate ourselves to be Numero Uno.

Collins's list of qualities of Level 5 leaders feels like a blend of the best of Confucian and Christian values:

- "demonstrates a compelling modesty . . . never boastful" ("Love is patient, love is kind. It does not envy, it does not boast, it is not proud" [1 Cor 13:4])

- "shunning public adulation" ("the nail that sticks out gets nailed down")

- "channels ambition into the company" (the group's success is more important than personal achievement)

- "sets up successors for even more greatness in the next generation" ("And what you have heard from me through many witnesses entrust to faithful people who will be able to teach others" [2 Tim 2:2 NRSV])

- "creates superb results" ("Do your best to present yourself to God as one approved by him, a worker who has no need to be ashamed, rightly explaining the word of truth" [2 Tim 2:15 NRSV])

- "demonstrates an unwavering resolve to do whatever must be done to produce the best long-term results, no matter how difficult" ("Whatever your task, put yourselves into it, as done for the Lord and not for your masters, since you know that from the Lord you will receive the inheritance as your reward; you serve the Lord Christ" [Col 3:23-24 NRSV])

When I scrutinize these two lists, the faces of several outstanding

Asian American leaders flash on my mental screen. When Collins fleshes out Level 5 leaders with Darwin Smith at Kimberly-Clark, Colman Mockler at Gillette, George Cain at Abbott Laboratories, Charles "Cork" Walgreen III at Walgreens, I can easily substitute them with the names of these Asian American leaders. And make no mistake, some of those names belong to remarkable *women*.

Here of course is the painful rub: the marketplace and the church hasn't yet caught on to what Collins has discovered. It may be a decade or two before headhunters and search committees get it. Some may never get it. Others may get it but refuse to change, to their great loss.

Meanwhile, we stay on task developing young leaders.

PROFILE OF A LEVEL 5 LEADER: JEANETTE YEP

Jeanette Yep is a Level 5 leader. She embodies Collins's Personal Humility/Professional Will checklist. Yep is InterVarsity Christian Fellowship's vice president of multiethnic ministry. For twenty-five years, she has served and led college students, campus ministers and their supervisors. What's most impressive about her career is the fruit her work has produced.

While serving as a staff director in Chicago in the '80s and '90s, she birthed and developed a strong ministry to Asian American students in Chicagoland. Her strategy was to not center it in her personality but to raise up young Asian American staff who could work closely with Asian American students. Peter Cha, now a professor at Trinity Evangelical

Divinity School; Jonathan Wu, a pastor at Evergreen Baptist Church of Los Angeles; and Greg Jao, divisional director of InterVarsity in Chicago, are but three of the staff Yep mentored and developed. Collins's descriptor "sets up successors for even more greatness in the next generation" fits Yep to a T.

She has also played key national roles, serving on committees to appoint presidents and vice presidents, and as a national field director overseeing the campus ministry. Her commitment to church ministry has never wavered. She is one of the founders of Parkwood Community Church, Chicago's first Asian American church.

A PLAN TO DEVELOP LEVEL 5 ASIAN AMERICAN LEADERS

As of this writing, InterVarsity employs 1,260 staff who work with 32,000 students. Of these, 115 staff and 4,000 students are Asian American, which means one of every eleven staff and one of every eight students in InterVarsity is an Asian American.

However, at the senior leadership level, Asian Americans are underrepresented. Jeanette Yep is the only Asian American vice president, and currently no regional directors are Asian Americans.

Regional directors are the key decision makers in InterVarsity. There are fourteen regions, with each regional director on the average overseeing five area directors, sixty-five campus staff and 2,360 students. Without exception, current regional directors previously served as area directors. Thus, if we are to have Asian American regional directors, we must cultivate Asian American area directors. Our plan for this is called the Daniel Project.

The Daniel Project aims to handpick and personally train, mentor and develop five current and nine potential Asian American area directors, with the goal of appointing at least five more area directors. We hope that perhaps three of these seven will eventually be asked to become a regional director, vice president or president of InterVarsity.

The goal is not to be politically correct or to fill quotas. Rather, it's our humble assumption that for InterVarsity to become a truly "great" multiethnic organization, it needs ethnic minority senior leaders, some being Asian American. Some of these potentially great leaders may go untapped because they don't fit the prevailing prototype of a top leader.

We currently employ dozens of gifted young Asian American staff with that paradoxical blend of "personal humility and professional will." With careful guidance, mentoring and training, some of these can become "great" senior leaders. The Daniel Project will enable us to offer InterVarsity our very best.

COUNTING THE COST OF BECOMING A LEVEL 5 LEADER

Perhaps as you've read through Collins's two charts describing Level 5 leaders, you've wondered about yourself. "Am I?" You feel a bit like Neo in *The Matrix*. You see some match-ups and wonder about a few others. Now what?

First off, relax. You're not being asked to save the world like Neo or Jesus. Level 5 leadership is not like a crown looking for the proper head to sit on. Rather, it's descriptive of those who are truly great leaders.

Next, if some of the qualities mentioned describe you, let them be affirmations of traits needed in outstanding leaders rather than an unbearable yoke to weigh you down.

Keep serving and leading well. Your Level 5 leadership qualities are good for those under your care and for the organizations in which you are a leader.

THE DANIEL PROJECT

In Daniel 1, Babylonian King Nebuchadnezzar chose young Jewish exiles with outstanding leadership potential. "They were trained for three years, and after that they were to enter the king's service" (Dan 1:5). Four of these came from Judah— Daniel and three friends.

The Daniel Project will accept a class of fourteen young Asian American staff who will attend:

- *a weeklong Asian American leadership development program*

- *a consultation weekend with a senior Asian American leader*

- *two consultations with their hand-picked senior staff mentor*

- *an on-site consultation with an area director in another part of the country*

- *proposals for placement in leadership roles*

While InterVarsity offers an excellent, two-year, new area-director training program, The Daniel Project will address issues not covered, such as succeeding as a minority in a majority culture organization, ethnic identity issues, maximizing Asian American qualities in leadership, shepherding and developing young Asian American staff and student leaders, and spiritual development as Asian American leaders.

The short-term results will be fourteen young, gifted leaders who will have had the best Asian American resources made available to them. Wherever they end up, they will be stronger and more effective leaders.

We will also continue to work the other end—helping our national leaders see the importance of having Asian Americans in top leadership roles.

Ask yourself, *Can I see myself in this organization for a long time?* If yes—meaning you feel good about the mission of the organization and that you have contributions to make—try to stay put for a significant amount of time. If you stay with the church, ministry or company for say, twenty years, you'll likely have a variety of different roles during that span of time. That's okay and healthy. We all change and we all need change. Staying long-term creates internal organizational stability. No ministry can succeed beyond a few generations without a good handful of long-haul decision makers.

TRANSITIONING WELL

When you find yourself in transition either from joining a new organization or being promoted internally, be prepared for change and perhaps to change. Being Asian American and taking on new leadership responsibilities will be costly, at the least, in these ways:

Especially in the transition from the former leader to you, learn two phrases and use them frequently: "I'm sorry (. . . you've been hurt"; . . . you feel that way"; . . . things have been hard for you here") and "*I don't know* but I'll try to find out." This is a critical time to build bridges and mend fences. Being heard and understood is paramount to most.

Invariably, you will hear criticism of your predecessor, no matter how beloved she or he was, especially if their leadership style was quite different than yours. Acknowledge the criticism but avoid affirming it.

If you are replacing a non-Asian American, expect your ethnicity to be an issue for those watching you. "Well, she's Asian American; they do things that way." Expect to run up against Asian stereotypes. Try to decide ahead of time how you will handle them.

Be decisive and verbal. One such stereotype is that we like to keep our own counsel, that we hold our cards close to our chest, that we are non-communicative and difficult to read. If that describes you, you will need to be unusually decisive and proactive in clearly verbalizing your positions on various issues. This may feel awkward for you but push yourself to keep doing it. The payoffs come later.

How you will be viewed and treated during your tenure can hinge on what kind of leader you are perceived to be during your first few months. The wet concrete of perception dries quickly. Don't blow it.

Be ready to have your leadership questioned. You represent a new paradigm of leadership. Some of the old guard won't paradigmatically shift, especially if they were loyal to your predecessor. They might not even shuffle your way. You might hear criticism and feel their lack of support. If you care a lot about what others think of you, this could throw you for a severe loop. Figure out organizationally whose opinions need to be heard well and heeded. Try to not let criticism from those not on that mental list penetrate deeply.

Stay focused on the mission and don't get preoccupied by how *you achieve* it. Achievement looks different in every leader. Your style of leadership may look like nothing ever seen in a senior leader in your fellowship, church or company. Mature on-lookers will understand, affirm you and translate you to others. They're your lifesavers, stay close to them.

Like Darwin Smith, *hold on to a few things that keep you rooted.* For Smith, it was continuing to hang out with plumbers and electricians and digging holes and moving rocks with his backhoe on his Wisconsin farm. Figure out who your "plumbers and electricians" are and what your backhoe is.

So, ye potential Level Fiver, is it worth it? If the mission is worth living for and dying for, then yes, yes, yes! Just say no to *shikata ga nai.* It *can* be helped! It *doesn't* have to be!

DEVELOPING AND
DEPLOYING ASIAN
AMERICAN LEADERS

THE UNIQUE MISSION OF ASIAN AMERICAN CHRISTIANS

Section two is written primarily for "leaders of the leaders"—those with mentoring and supervisory responsibilities for the emerging generations of Asian American leaders—the "uncles" and "aunties," big brothers and sisters or just plain bosses. Some of you will be Asian American, others something else. The most well-rounded young leaders will have mentors and leaders of varying hues.

JESUS AND THE ASIAN AMERICAN CHURCH

At the risk of heresy:

"I, John, was in the Spirit on the Lord's Day, and I heard behind me a loud voice like a trumpet saying, 'Write in a book what you see and send it to the churches of Asian heritage in America—to the Korean American church, to the Vietnamese American church, to the Chinese American church, to the Japanese American church, to the Pakistani American church, to the Indian American church, to the Filipino American church, to those Asian American believers in predominantly white churches, to those of mixed racial heritage—here is what I have to say to you in the early twenty-first century . . ."

What would Jesus say through his oracle, John, to Asian American Christians? As in Revelation 2—3, what qualities would he applaud? In what areas of deficiency or sin would he proclaim judgment? I am not Jesus, to be sure, but let me take a stab at it.

I believe Jesus would affirm our tenacity in being faithful in the midst of huge cultural adjustments and challenges. I believe he would acknowledge the sacrifices made by the first and second generations for the sake of both their family and their immigrant church. I believe he would congratulate us for usually not retaliating when attacked by racists and bigots. I believe he would credit us for our concern for our people back in our motherlands as we pray, send money and visit.

But after kudos would come critique. Much like he did for the seven churches addressed in Revelation, he would give it not as final judgment but fair warning. His love for these churches ran so deep that he pointed out their worst offenses and liabilities because he wanted the very best for them.

> I reprove and discipline those whom I love. Be earnest, therefore, and repent. Listen! I am standing at the door, knocking; if you hear my voice and open the door, I will come in to you and eat with you, and you with me. (Rev 3:19-20 NRSV)

There is both grace and time for repentance and change.

With all my heart, I believe Asian American Christians can make a huge difference not just within our own communities but beyond—in other communities of faith, in American society and around the globe. But it won't come naturally to us when he tells us the truth about ourselves and nudges us out of our comfort zones.

Here is my dream, what I would love to see written to us:

"I, John, was in the Spirit on the Lord's Day, and I heard behind me a loud voice like a trumpet saying, 'Write in a book what you see and send it to the churches of Asian heritage in America:

'To the Filipino American church, amidst the remnants of the evils of colonialism, the love-hate relationship America has with your people, and the ways you have been separated from your kapwa pilipino *(fellow Filipino) and your* pamilya *(family) in pursuit of the American dream, your faithful struggle and sacrificial love has birthed a generation of people who know how to celebrate life and are gifted in crosscultural mission, hospitality and performance;*

'To the Vietnamese American church, you have risen above the suffering and sadness of your young history; you have been the misunderstood outsider, penalized for atrocities not your doing;

'To the Korean American church, you stopped fighting among yourselves,

which let petty differences create far too many churches; you woke up to see how much you had to offer non-Korean American Christians—so much that some of your churches partnered with other churches to form pan-Asian and even multiethnic churches; you developed trusting friendships with African Americans; you were used by God to somehow help bring North and South Korea together as nations; you allowed Jesus to transform your spirit of triumphalism to one of servanthood;

'To the Japanese American church, you allowed Jesus to heal the deep, damaging wounds brought on by the internment of your ancestors and you chose to find your identity in him and not in "camp"; you didn't see your wealth as your compensation for "camp" but as God's blessing to share with others; you created a place for your many hapa (biracial) children who didn't sense they were completely bona fide and welcome;

'To the Chinese American church, you released your children so they felt free to pursue God's leading for their vocations, which allowed some of them to become missionaries and pastors, others to work in service and nonprofit sectors, others to pursue the arts; instead of letting the gap between overseas-born (OBCs) and American-born Chinese (ABCs) widen, you kept communicating and working hard so your appreciation for each other deepened;

'To the pan-Asian American church, you overcame historical differences between nationalities to attain authentic oneness in Christ, where each nationality represented was affirmed and its uniqueness celebrated;

'To all, you stopped hoarding your gifts and talents from the broader Christian family, turning your church communities and fellowships into ethnic ghettoes with invisible signage that clearly states, "Stay Away";

'For those blessed with wealth, you didn't automatically attribute it to hard work alone, but saw it as God's blessing; you didn't instinctively look for the best house, car and children's education that your money could buy; you were thoughtful in funding strategic endeavors that built up the kingdom of God;

'You shut down the vicious downward spiral of self-hatred, of despising your Asianness and doubting your life can make any difference outside of your ethnic community; believing that God didn't make a mistake when you were made Asian and you have a unique destiny and purpose.'"

I HAVE DREAMS

I dream of and long for the day when

- every one of the twelve million Asian Americans has had the gospel shared with them in a culturally relevant way that allows them to make a choice for or against following Jesus

- along with the First African Methodist Episcopal Church and the First Korean Methodist Church four blocks away, there would also be a merged Very First African-Korean American Methodist Church that is known as a leader in community reconciliation

- immigrant churches have mentoring and leadership development programs so they feel very comfortable handing the baton of leadership to the next generation

- parachurch campus ministries like Asian American Christian Fellowship, InterVarsity and the Navigators have earned the trust and respect of Asian American church leaders so we become true partners and not competitors

- Asian American Christian leaders in California, *where one-third of all Asian Americans reside*, link arms and partner together to reach these 4.3 million Asian Americans with the gospel (by 2025, it is projected there will be 9.1 million Asian Americans in California)

- each of the five cities with the largest Asian American populations (New York City, Los Angeles, San Jose, San Francisco and Honolulu) have Asian American church leaders who take seriously the mandate "to whom much has been give will much be expected" as they seek to serve these large Asian American population centers

- the Japanese American Citizens League (JACL), Organization of Chinese Americans (OCA), Korean American Coalition (KAC), *AsianWeek* and other leading Asian American voices look to Asian American churches and believers for leadership, especially in the areas of spiritual development, diversity issues, justice and racial reconciliation

- the U.S. president calls on Asian American church leaders along with leaders of secular organizations like JACL and OCA when crises arise in our communities

- Asian American churches have evangelism, discipleship and mentoring plans for the huge mission field of young Asian Americans (29 percent of Asian Americans in 1999—3.7 million—were under twenty-five)
- East Asian American believers recognize Indian American and Pakistani Americans as fellow Asian Americans and welcome them into their fellowships and churches, that the invitation is made even if they choose not to join
- our Asian American sisters are respected more and given the same leadership opportunities as men
- Asian Americans value their contributions, speak up and be more assertive in non-Asian American gatherings
- we value risk-taking more than conformity, saying no to the mantra that the nail that sticks out is meant to be nailed down

These are my dreams. If they are of God, may we agree, "Lord, may they be so."

PUTTING FEET TO DREAMS

In order to keep, cultivate and serve young Asian Americans, here is what I believe is needed in the two major arenas, Asian American churches and fellowships and multiethnic churches and fellowships.

For Asian American churches and fellowships:

- if in an nationality-specific church or fellowship, develop a clearly articulated mission statement and what role young Asian Americans might have in accomplishing it
- if that can't or won't happen, then empower and bless young leaders to form Asian American churches to reach their generation
- help them understand and appreciate their ethnic identity (surprisingly, little is done in most Asian American churches and fellowships)
- provide high-level discipleship and leadership training that affirms and

engages their ethnic identity rather than training

- empower them to pursue the unique role of Asian Americans in racial reconciliation
- help them appreciate and respect Asian Americans who choose to be in multiethnic churches and fellowships

For Asian Americans active in multiethnic churches and fellowships:

- help them embrace diversity and affirm differences
- let them lead, even when their leadership style is different than others'
- affirm their being Asian American and create a safe place to discuss ethnicity
- make racial reconciliation a high priority
- adopt unique strategies in evangelizing ethnic communities
- help them appreciate and respect Asian Americans who choose to be in Asian American churches and fellowships

Clearly, the next fifteen to twenty-five years will be a period of extraordinary opportunities for Asian American believers to impact our world. You are in a unique position as a mentor or leader of emerging Asian American leaders to help them make history. Come join the party! You are warmly invited to lead those who lead.

BIG NUMBERS THAT BREATHE AND BLEED

If our dreams are to come true, they need to be based on reality. But because Asian America is morphing at near warp speed, it's impossible to get it to move in "bullet time"—slowly enough to examine it. As soon as I think I understand some trends or patterns, they change. I trust that at least the broader brushstrokes of principles will remain true. If you are someone's Yoda, part of your role is to grasp these brushstrokes, explain them and point your Luke in directions that matter for eternity.

WHAT CENSUS 2000 MEANS FOR ASIAN AMERICANS

When we say Asian America in the early twenty-first century isn't quite like it was in 1960, we're not comparing tangerines to tangelos. It's more like grapefruit to tangelo—similar textured outer peel, citrus pulp and seeds, and that's it. That's how much Asian America has changed and keeps evolving.

In *The Matrix* the hero, Neo, is hounded by bad guys who in a flash change their appearance to battle him more effectively. Asian America today seems to be changing almost as quickly. It's hard to keep up. Blink, it's different.

One major way Asian America is growing is in sheer numbers.[1] Figure 11.1 illustrates our growth between 1970 and 2000.

One new law changed the face of America forever. The Immigration and Nationality Act of 1965 abolished the national-origins quotas and provided for the annual admission of 170,000 immigrants from the Eastern Hemisphere (20,000 per country) as well as 120,000 from the Western Hemisphere. The doors to America flung open and haven't shut since. Figure 11.2 illustrates the composition of the Asian American family in 1960, 1985 and 2000 (showing the largest groups).

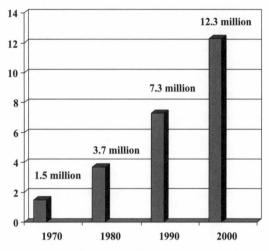

Figure 11.1. Asian American population (overall)

In 1960 we were half of one percent of the entire U.S. population, meaning one of every two hundred Americans was of Asian ancestry. Breaking that .5 percent down, the Asian American family in 1960 was

52 percent Japanese

27 percent Chinese

20 percent Filipino

1 percent Korean

1 percent Indian

Twenty-five years later in 1985 we had quadrupled in number, making up 2.1 percent of the U.S. population with

21 percent Chinese

21 percent Filipino

15 percent Japanese

12 percent Vietnamese

11 percent Korean

10 percent Indian
4 percent Laotian
3 percent Cambodian
3 percent other Asian Americans

In the next fifteen years, from 1985 to 2000, we more than doubled, becoming 4.5 percent of the U.S. population, close to one of every twenty Americans being of Asian ancestry (see figure 11.4). The breakdown:[2]

24 percent Chinese
18 percent Filipino
16 percent Indian
11 percent Vietnamese
11 percent Korean
8 percent Japanese
4 percent Native Hawaiian and other Pacific Islanders

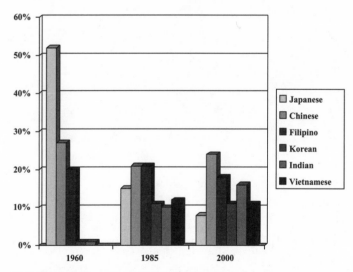

Figure 11.2. Asian American population by ethnic origin

What's striking is the dramatic decline of Japanese Americans (see figure 11.3). Once 52 percent of all Asian Americans in 1960, Japanese Americans comprised only 8 percent in 2000. The table now seats Korean

Americans, Vietnamese Americans and Indian Americans in their place. Significant immigration from Japan hasn't happened in decades. Additionally, Japanese Americans marry out more than any other ethnic group and many of their progeny are choosing to not identify themselves as Asian Americans in the census. Organizations like the Japanese American Citizens League are struggling for a corporate identity and purpose.

Currently, one-fourth of all foreign-born residents are from Asia. Projections made from the 2000 census for the next forty years forecast Asian Americans to become 8 percent of the U.S. population (one of every twelve) by 2040.

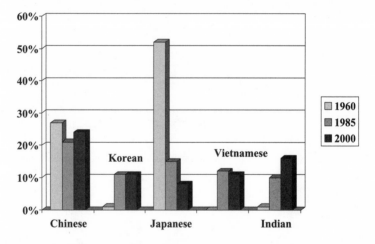

Figure 11.3. The changing face of Asian America

1990 TO 2000: HUGE HUE CHANGES IN ASIAN AMERICA

From 1990 to 2000 alone, dramatic changes have taken place. There has been an increase from 7.3 million to 12.3 million Asian Americans. We grew 69 percent, the largest percentage increase of all racial groups for that period.

The six nationalities with the fastest rate of growth were from South Asia and Southeast Asia. South Asian Americans doubled between 1990 and

2000, with Vietnamese Americans not far behind, increasing by 83 percent. *There are now more South and Southeast Asian Americans combined than those of East Asian heritage.* The days of ministering to the Wongs, Sakamotos and Kims only are behind us forever. The "browning" of Asian America is here.

The largest numerical growth were in the Indian American and Chinese American communities, which added 864,000 and 741,000 respectively. (For complete statistics of growth in the various Asian American communities between 1990 and 2000, see the chart in the appendix.)

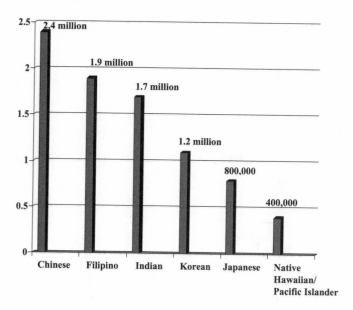

Figure 11.4. Asian Americans by nationality, 2000

While our numerical growth has been strong, especially among South Asian Americans, we're still a thin slice of the American population pie. As Figure 11.5 shows, in 2000, Asian Americans made up 4.5 percent of the U.S. population, the rest of which were 68.5 percent white, 13 percent African American, 12.5 percent Hispanic American and 1.5 percent Native American. One of 22 Americans is of Asian ancestry.

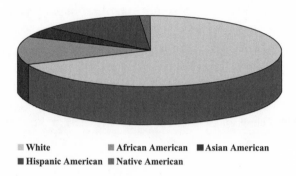

■ White   ■ African American   ■ Asian American
■ Hispanic American   ■ Native American

Figure 11.5. U.S. population by race, 2000 census

Another dramatic shift taking place is where Asian Americans choose to live. Historically, many of the earliest Asian Americans came as farmers but no longer. In 2000, 46 percent of all Asian Americans lived in the central cities and 49 percent were found in the suburbs.

One of every two Asian Americans live in the West (see figure 11.6). One of every eight Californians is Asian American. California alone accounts for 36 percent of all Asian Americans in the United States.

Figure 11.6. Where Asian Americans live, 2000

The numerical growth of Asian Americans can be viewed in at least two ways: (1) increase in the *number* of Asian Americans, and (2) the *percentage* increase of Asian Americans.

More than half—2.9 million of 5 million new Asian Americans between 1990 and 2000—chose to live in five states: California, New York, Texas, Hawaii and New Jersey (see figure 11.7).

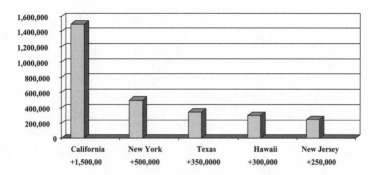

Figure 11.7. Five states add 2.9 million Asian Americans, 1990-2000

While their numerical increases were not as large, there were ten states (figure 11.8) that experienced over 100 percent increases in the number of Asian Americans from 1990 to 2000. Why note these states? As members of an ethnic minority group, any time "our people" doubles or triples in size where we live, we feel it. Make no mistake: those not in our ethnic community also notice and feel it, when newcomers of a different tone come to roost on land that had for decades been theirs.

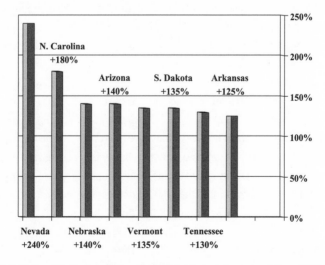

Figure 11.8. States with the largest increases of Asian American population, 1990-2000

BIG ASIAN AMERICAN NUMBERS: NOW WHAT?

Seeing all these numbers impacts me the way seeing that first big wave did when I used to bodysurf at Santa Cruz in northern California. "Whoa, time to go home!" After getting over the initial shock of its size and potential impact on my body, I'd take a deep breath and paddle out and *become one with the waves*. Well, sort of.

Let's breathe deeply and look at the possible implications for ministry to Asian Americans. When we crunch numbers we must always remember that each number breathes, bleeds and represents a person who is loved by God and is deserving of our love as well.

The first implication is we'll continue to need immigrant churches. Currently, one fourth (6.1 million) of all foreign-born residents are from Asia. As I drive around Atlanta, almost every medium to large church has a fairly new-looking sign up—advertising a new Korean, Hmong, Vietnamese or Cambodian (or Haitian, Bosnian or Sudanese—you name it) congregation. Many that have made it past the initial phases have their own facility.

Unless immigration laws change dramatically, the need continues for specialized ministries to reach and serve first-generation immigrants. If these start-up churches didn't exist, many of their members would not attend church and myriad seekers would not have a comfortable place to explore the Christian faith.

God used and still uses nationality-focused churches to sustain the first and second generations. For many of them, their church is their lifeline, ethnically, socially and spiritually. It's the one place where they can go for sustenance. The mother tongue is spoken, the food at potlucks is their soul food, everyone there looks like them. It's home.

The immigrant church is not for everyone. It may not be for us, but let's be sure to honor and bless it and pray that many first and second generation folk will be reached there because they may not be reachable any other way.

Two, we have "family members" who don't know they are in the family, others who don't want to be in the family, others that we don't consider a part of the family. The U.S. Census Bureau's definition of *Asian American* is "a person having origins in any of the original peoples of the Far East, Southeast Asia, or the Indian subcontinent." This definition works for them in counting numbers, but it doesn't work in describing a large family or community that owns and is committed to each other.

It's incredibly difficult to build a church or campus fellowship that is inclusive of the broad family of all Asian Americans. I haven't seen it happen yet over a sustained period of time. I'm not sure it can happen in the next ten to fifteen years. We are that different. I think we should keep trying, if that's the vision God has given us, but it won't be easy.

For those of us of the East Asian persuasion, we're usually comfortable enough with each other. We're even okay with stretching the boundaries to include Southeast Asians. Where it gets awkward is with South Asians and perhaps Native Hawaiians and Pacific Islanders.

Let me be totally honest. When I'm with an Indian American I don't naturally think *fellow Asian American* like I do with a Chinese American or Vietnamese American. I'm thinking, *Are you really one of us? Do you even want to be one of us?* It takes a lot of work to be family when our physical appearance and customs are quite different. I can choose to be a host or a stranger when thinks get awkward or my world gets threatened.

As leaders we set a tone of inclusivity or exclusivity by whom we invite into our fellowships and especially into leadership roles. We don't have to say a word against a particular people group; if we don't include them, we have made a strong statement. *Not to decide is to decide.*

The third implication is helping adopted Asian Americans affirm their ethnic identity and not see themselves as the same race as their adoptive family. My heart breaks every time I hear of an adopted Asian American college student or young adult who was raised to be like their adoptive family, in most cases, white. Often, they are angry, confused and feel betrayed. Such families need to seek a healthy balance of affirming their child's unique ethnicity while helping them assimilate into their family.

Fourth, we need to help our churches and fellowships warmly receive interracial couples and their biracial children just as they do Asian American couples and children. The 2000 census was the first census that made it possible to check more than one racial category, with 6.8 million (2.4 percent of the total population) doing so. One only has to study the child and teen models in department store ads to see how marketers read the winds of change. Their ads tell us, "We know you are out there."

Biracial and multiracial children of interracial marriages are a large and rapidly growing minority group and can no longer be treated as a footnote or afterthought. One-third of all biracial or multiracial people in 2000 were biracial or multiracial Asians—Asian and at least one other ethnicity (2.1 million of the 6.8 million). To put that in perspective, the largest Asian American group is Chinese Americans with 2.4 million. *After them, biracial and multiracial Asian Americans are the second largest Asian American group!*

What will Asian America look like in 2025? Most likely a lot like what Japanese Americans, especially in California, look like in 2002. Japanese Americans marry out more than any other ethnic minority group. In California, fifth-generation Japanese Americans are arriving in force. Their great-great grandparents came to America at the start of the twentieth century and their experience in the internment camps accelerated the assimilation process of their children. One of the outcomes of assimilating was marrying those we were trying to be like.

BEING BIRACIAL: HALF AS GOOD OR TWICE BETTER?

All of us need to confront honestly our true feelings about those with biracial backgrounds. To us, are they "half as good" or "twice better"? Do we see them as offering a unique perspective because of their living in two worlds or do we feel they only have half as much to offer because they are not fully in either world? Can we give them a unique place of ministry as "bridge people" between the two communities?

Because of their growing numbers, multiracial people are too numerous to be ignored or denied. Generation Xers and the Millennials tend to embrace those with biracial identity. Older generations—boomers and the Silent Generation—are slower to welcome them into their churches and families.

In *Pursuing the Pearl*, Ken Fong cites "four generalizations" about interracial marriages involving Asian Americans[3]:

- Japanese Americans marry out more than any other Asian American group as well as all other ethnic minorities.

- The length of time an Asian group has been here is directly correlated to the incidence of intermarriage.

- Other factors, such as how a group has been culturally programmed to deal with changes or adaptation, may also play a significant role in the incidence of intermarriages.

- Females consistently marry out at a higher rate than males.

The following questions might be helpful as we explore our openness to this new Asian American "nationality":

- Are there other races or Asian nationalities in particular that are not warmly received as visitors, members, potential leaders? Is it because we're afraid that ultimately they might marry one of "our own"?

- Are we open to having our "best and brightest" children of the church marry someone of another nationality?

- How do we treat the non-Asian American in a biracial relationship?

- Are those in interracial marriages and their children viewed as full-fledged members, just as all others?

Grandparents are in a special position to bless or curse their biracial or multiracial grandchildren. I have seen both take place, one getting their sense of place in the family blasted away, the other basking in that special love and security grandparents give. *You really are a part of this family* is the message of a grandmother's or grandfather's embrace. Our biracial son, Sam, has received that embrace from all of his grandparents and the fruit is evident.

HOW DO NON-ASIAN AMERICANS VIEW ASIAN AMERICA?

Up until the 1990s, InterVarsity's triennial missions convention was a mostly white gathering. Then Korean American churches decided to send their students to Urbana '90, and it hasn't been the same since.

Urbana 2000 gave us a snapshot of the future. Urbana 2000 was 26 percent Asian American (plus 9 percent other minorities). Consider the white student from South Dakota or Wyoming as she steps into the main meeting hall with 20,000 delegates. She looks around. *Wham!* It doesn't look 26 percent Asian American to her. It probably looks at least 50 percent. She might think, *No one told me that Urbana is an Asian American conference!*

During day one she struggles to feel at home. *Am I welcome here? Is this conference for me?* she wonders. How Asian Americans treat her that first day is critical to her comfort level for the rest of the conference. Will we "clump" or "unclump" and welcome her to "our" party?

The call for believers to be hospitable and welcoming runs throughout Scripture. The Asian American presence at Urbana 2000 was a sneak preview of what life in America will be like in this new millennium. Woe to us if we keep clumping.

The Committee of 100 is a group of over one hundred prominent Chinese Americans working on promoting the full participation of Chinese Americans in American life. In May 2001, following the release of the 2000 census findings, they produced the results of their extensive survey on "American Attitudes Towards Chinese Americans and Asian Americans." Like Urbana, it is another revealing snapshot.

The study is both fascinating and disturbing. It found that the majority of Americans admire Chinese Americans' strong family values, their honesty as businesspeople, see them being as patriotic as other Americans and placing a higher value on education than do most other groups in America. It also reported unsettling findings:

- 46 percent believe that Chinese Americans passing on secret information to the Chinese government is a problem
- 34 percent feel Chinese Americans have too much influence in the U.S. high technology sector
- 32 percent feel Chinese Americans always like to be at the head of things
- 32 percent feel Chinese Americans are more loyal to China than to the United States
- 21 percent feel Chinese Americans don't care what happens to anyone but their own kind

Most disturbing was that the study indicated that 25 percent of all surveyed had "very negative attitudes and stereotypes of Chinese Americans."

The prejudices of this group center on beliefs that Chinese Americans

- are more loyal to China than to the United States: 87 percent
- have too much influence in the U.S. high technology sector: 82 percent
- always like to be at the head of things: 81 percent
- believe that Chinese Americans passing on secret information to the Chinese government is a problem: 75 percent
- see the increase of the Asian population as being bad for the United States: 57 percent

And lest those of us not Chinese American feel we're off the hook, the study reveals that *most non-Asian Americans couldn't tell the difference between Chinese Americans and other Asian Americans and registered similar percentages about other Asian Americans.*

As Asian Americans continue to increase in numbers, influence and economic clout, expect these percentages to rise. "But these perceptions aren't accurate!" is not as important as the fact that a lot of people have them. Ministry needs to be done in light of prevailing—not wished-for—perceptions.

ASIAN AMERICAN CORPORATE CULTURE

Those of us in organizational leadership roles have the opportunity *to create corporate cultures that are Asian American-friendly.* Clearly, some organizations are better than others as places where Asian Americans can lead well within.

When those values become part of the corporate DNA, structural changes will naturally flow out of them. In time, the organization will have

- Asian Americans in mid-to-senior-level management (and not limited to "diversity" positions)
- a respectable number of Asian American board members
- non-Asian American board members and senior leaders advocating for Asian Americans with some serving as their personal mentors
- long-range plans that call for recruitment and integral involvement of Asian Americans at all levels

GOOD ORGANIZATIONS FOR ASIAN AMERICAN LEADERS*

- *are self-aware about different leadership styles (i.e., direct-indirect, male-female, loud-quiet, assertive-deferential)*

- *value and openly discuss different styles*

- *at the top levels, have a variety of leadership styles*

- *value "processing" as much as making the decision*

- *develop minority viewpoints and styles of expression*

- *have a corporate ethos that encourages diversity and multiethnicity throughout the entire*

organization, not just for those who are "into it"; it's a place where ethnicity and ethnic identity issues are affirmed

- *have top leaders who have an awareness of institutional and systemic injustice within their organization and are doing something about it*

- *are willing to fund training opportunities and cross-pollination for Asian American leaders with other Asian American or minority leaders—inside and outside the organization*

* Greg Jao, a seasoned leader at Parkwood Community Church in Chicago and in InterVarsity contributed heavily to this list.

- a good track record of retaining Asian American personnel

Conversely, "Asian American unfriendly" organizations will likely have

- no Asian Americans in at least middle management positions

- no Asian American board members

- no possible advocates or mentors who have a good understanding of Asian Americans

- poor funding for training and development of Asian Americans in leadership roles

- nothing or very little in the long-range plan for recruitment and development of Asian American leaders

- senior leaders who call Asian Americans "Orientals" or Asians, and don't recognize them as Americans

- a majority culture ethos with little hope or interest in changing; ethnicity and ethnic identity issues are ignored or bad-mouthed
- a poor track record of retaining Asian American personnel

I find it helpful to ask, Who in the organization has the authority to change the corporate culture? And what would partnering with this person or group look like?

CALIFORNIA DREAMING

Soon after James Marshall discovered gold at Sutter's Mill in 1848, Chinese came in droves to Gam Saan, "gold mountain" as they nicknamed California. A mere four years later, Chinese made up ten percent of the entire population of California. One hundred and fifty years later, California is still our Gam Saan. As we plan for the future, we need to become more strategic about California. Here's why we need to keep looking westward: it has the largest number of Asian Americans of any state; it continues to attract large numbers of the "newer" Asian Americans, thus the rest of the country can learn from them; almost as a reflex, we look to California as the trendsetters (for things good or tacky).

At Urbana '93 I led a workshop for Asian American pastors and church leaders. A fascinating discussion emerged with ideas and struggles thrown back and forth. As I stood back and watched, I saw two groups taking shape by the things they shared. One group was those from California. The other group was almost everyone else. The ideas shared were that distinct.

At the end, I made some concluding remarks. I said to East Coast leaders, "You may not like everything shared by the California pastors. But we need to listen carefully because the issues they are wrestling with now will be coming your way in ten years or so."

I still believe that. California has the oldest history of significant numbers of Asian Americans. As some of them are now into their fifth and even sixth generations, those in Chicago, St. Louis, Houston, Atlanta, Ann Arbor, Raleigh, D.C., New Brunswick, New York City, Philadelphia and Boston would do well to see what California churches and fellowships are doing and learning.

We should take notes, however, with a caveat—because California is its own very unique planet, we should not try to replicate what's being done there. We would be wise to take principles and apply them to our unique context. What works great in Berkeley may not fly in St. Louis or Pittsburgh. But let's set aside our California stereotypes and jokes and learn from our laid-back brothers and sisters. Dude, they are paving the way for the rest of us.

THE LATINO FUTURE

Another major implication of Census 2000 is *estamos llegando al punto de ser un pais Latino: we are becoming an Hispanic country*. Let's face the music; most Asian Americans are extremely prejudiced. We look down on those who are not as educated and fluent in English as we are. While we may not verbalize that we picked up ourselves by our bootstraps, we are condescending to those minorities who haven't achieved as much as we have. We've made it on our own, why can't they?

We are becoming a Hispanic country, and we need to see Hispanic Americans as friends, not as enemies or invisible people. We see this change almost everywhere in the country. It is forecasted that by 2005, Hispanic Americans will pass African Americans and become the largest ethnic minority, making up over 13 percent of the U.S. population. One of every eight Americans will be Hispanic. That trend will continue: by 2050, one of every three Americans will be Hispanic.

Unless there are major changes to immigration law, by 2025, certainly by 2050, we could rename the United States the United Latino States of America. Because much of the growth is through immigration, the immigrants' first language will be Spanish. Our public education system will likely make Spanish the mandatory foreign language all children are taught. Speaking Spanish will need to become almost second nature.

Signage will keep changing. Our broken Spanish learned years ago in high school won't do. My gut response is, "Come on, you're in America, speak English!" That may make me feel superior but it won't build relationships. My wife and I took a Spanish course last year as our side of Atlanta is becoming increasingly Hispanic.

The changes won't be limited to language or tons of new Latino restaurants. I grew up believing Latinos—especially Mexican Americans—were inferior to me. In recent years in Asian American circles, I've realized I am not alone. Many of us may need to repent of racism, prejudice and stereotypes toward Latinos who are in a lower socioeconomic bracket than us.

It has taken generations of blood, sweat, prayer, tears, repentance and civil rights legislation for African Americans to no longer be treated as slaves, visible chains or not. As Hispanics become a larger presence, we can expect a long, hard road to full-fledged citizenry to become reality.

What can we do? *As African Americans did the hard work in paving the way for themselves and other ethnic minorities—like us—can we do the same for Hispanic Americans?*

This is true leadership: looking out for the underdog and leading on their behalf, not just for the privileged who can fend for themselves. Then it means empowering their leadership.

Several years ago, Mario, a Mexican American in his twenties, moved from the Bay Area to Atlanta. He was befriended by Leo, a Chinese American who was attending Stanford and home for the summer. Leo had met Mario and brought him to Atlanta Chinese Christian Church. I held my breath during his first few weeks.

When Mario came to *my* church (and I'm not even Chinese American!) I had to confront my own ugly, selfish, racist thoughts of *What are you doing here?* Then I wondered if others would accept him. He joined the young adult fellowship, served on the ushering team and overall seemed to be welcomed. That's the picture I hope will be replicated over and over all across the country in our Asian American churches. When will we know they are fully accepted? When they date and perhaps marry the children of the church and the elders give their blessing.

THE *REALLY* BIG NUMBERS AND THE BOTTOM LINE

Census 2000 bulges with implications for all Americans, not just Asian Americans. But the magic year, say our national number crunchers, appears to be 2056 when European Americans will be less than 50 percent of the population. That has huge implications for ministry and more generally, life in America. *The year 2056 might inaugurate a bigger new millennium than the year 2000.*

Whatever ministry we do now, we must do it in light of demographics that are moving in one direction: *America is losing its white corporate face.*

What's going to happen when white America *in reality* becomes the minority around 2056? The disempowerment they will experience will not sit well with them. Whites have always had the upper hand, the position of power and prestige in America. To watch it slip away will be difficulty for many. Look for increasing outbursts of anger and frustration. Look for those who have taken their places at the table to be the immediate targets of the outbursts.

When power is lost, vision gets blurred and the enemy becomes those who don't look and act like me. The years ahead of us can either be a bad accident waiting to happen or a time of incredible opportunities to show America what the kingdom of God is meant to be like.

By thinking, planning and praying *now*, we might be able to prevent some ugly episodes down the road. It's important that kingdom people live out a different paradigm of power. It's not to be wrested from others and wielded over those with less. The more biblical model is *shared authority and responsibility*. We can also help our white brethren let go gracefully by embracing them and helping them understand what it is going to feel like being a minority.

Asian Americans need to step up and lead in the arena of racial reconciliation. Proactive leadership—now, not in 2056—is needed.

Robert Lamont, former president of the Presbyterian Ministers Fund, put it well: "A leader is someone who can sense the tide of events, who can look at the circumstances of the present and can translate them to the opportunities of the future." Forward-looking Asian American churches like NewSong in Irvine, California, Evergreen Baptist of Los Angeles and Cambridge Community Fellowship Church in Cambridge, Massachusetts, are warmly welcoming non-Asian Americans, especially other people of color.

Asian Americans cannot afford to allow our prominent default mode of fatalism to kick in as our modus operandi. We would do well to heed these warnings:

- Edmund Burke, the eighteenth-century British statesman and orator: "The only thing necessary for the triumph of evil is for good [people] to do nothing."

- Eugene Peterson in *Run with the Horses*: "Incalculable evil comes from those unlikely sources: quiet, little people doing their job, long since having given up thinking of themselves as responsible, moral individuals."[4]

- Herman Melville in *The Confidence-Man*: "The moderate man, the invaluable understopper of the wicked man. You the moderate man may be used for wrong, you are useless for right."[5]

Now is the time to be nails that stick out and not be pounded down. What is needed? Leaders who will

- teach biblically and frequently about God's love for all people, not just those who look like us

- stand up on behalf of ethnic minorities—of their own and other ethnicities—who are treated unjustly

- work alongside both Christian and secular leaders of other minority groups

- walk in the shoes of white Americans, working hard at understanding what it is like to be the minority for the first time (if anyone can do this well, it's us)

When racial walls grow taller or when race wars break out, we need to be prepared to be peacemakers, bridge-builders and agents of biblical shalom. While there is relative peace among the various ethnic groups, it is an uneasy peace at best. Such détente helps, but détente is not the same as shalom.

In times of economic prosperity, when there are plenty of decent jobs and money to go around, we maintain détente. When the economy falters so does détente. History shows we start looking hard at those who keep us from having what we believe is rightfully ours. In 2025, when two of every five citizens will be nonwhite, dividing walls will get thicker and taller. Whites will flee the suburbs for the exurbs at even a greater rate than now. Fear of those unlike them will only grow.

Well-trained, committed Asian American leaders can be useful in this landscape. Our basic commitment to public education has developed friendships and relational skills with other minorities. (Is it no wonder that the Asian American hip-hop movement is not derided but basically blessed by black hip-hoppers?) Presence is prerequisite to authentic leadership. We've been there, and I hope we will not flee.

At the same time, we've assimilated into the white world. We know how it works and how to be a part of it. This puts us in a unique place of standing as peacemakers between warring factions. I see within young Asian Americans a growing desire to be proactive peacemakers. I'm hopeful.

12

DIFFERENT, SOMETIMES WAY DIFFERENT

We are in the process of raising up the emerging generation of Asian American leaders. These young leaders will be extraordinary in their ability to navigate the ethnic realities of the twenty-first century. If you are called upon to develop, train, mentor them—you choose the verb—strap yourself in for a wonderful ride full of twists, turns, tunnels and adventure. At times we will see mirror reflections of these young leaders' parents but don't be fooled. They're blazing a very different pathway. Let them blaze.

Before you ask, "Where do I start?" or "How can I help?" having some understanding of the following will help you to serve them well:

- There is no such thing as Asian America.
- We're different, sometimes way different.
- Nobody's outreaching the unreached planet: unchurched Asian Americans.

NO ASIAN AMERICA

This may sound strange, but in a very real sense *there is no such thing as Asian America* and even Asian Americans. They are the media's inventions of the late '60s. Put a first generation Hmong American, a fifth generation biracial Japanese American and a second generation Pakistani American together in a room and tell them they are all the same. This would create one lively discussion—if they can understand each other. Broad labels have their place but care must be taken to use them with understanding.

A few lessons I've learned, usually the hard way:

- We're not a monolithic culture. We have no central Asian American headquarters, spokesperson, secret handshake or code of values to which we all subscribe.

- "Asian American" and "Asian Pacific American" are not terms most of us use to identify ourselves. Primarily we think of ourselves as Indian Americans, Korean Americans, Vietnamese Americans and so on. We "own" our own but are reluctant to feel the same about other Asian nationalities.

- We hate being stereotyped (unless we do it to ourselves!). LEAP's worksheet "Asian Pacific American Cultural Values" prefaces its list of values with the necessary caveats: "This is not a complete listing of Asian Pacific cultural values. Please do not use this list to further stereotype Asian Pacific Americans. Not every cultural value is applicable to every Asian Pacific group nor does each cultural value influence every Asian Pacific American equally. In addition, these cultural values are not exclusively Asian Pacific."

When I grew up in the Bay Area in the '50s and '60s, there was no Asian America. In my world, there were Japanese—and everyone else. True, I knew some Chinese Americans but I didn't consider them to be in my "immediate family." They were more like fourth cousins with odd one-syllable last names and food spicier than our own. Forays into San Francisco's Chinatown for Chinese New Year was an exotic crosscultural experience, not an opportunity to hang with the brothers and sisters.

In the early '70s, I learned there were Asian Americans and I was one. Owning that larger family meant I had to work hard on my prejudices and stereotypes. In-house Asian racism is often brutal and unforgiving.

My ethnocentric pecking order had Japanese Americans at the top, of course. Chinese Americans were second and Filipino Americans a distant third. Other Southeast Asian Americans, South Asian Americans and Korean Americans weren't even on my screen as family members.

GETTING TO KNOW US

When I am developing a relationship with another Asian American, I try to find out a variety of things (generally not in one sitting!). As a fellow Asian American, I'm allowed some "grace points" or family member's privilege that might not be given a non-Asian American. Don't fire off these questions rat-a-tat-tat like you are Jay Leno or Larry King interviewing Ang Lee or Margaret Cho. Know that behind some of these areas are pain, anger, struggles to forgive, and twenty more related questions. Build trust first, then ask with care and love.

- *Their nationality,* that is, Thai American, Pakistani American, Taiwanese American. I have embarrassed myself too many times by guessing wrongly. Now I ask.

- *Generation to which they belong.* Keep in mind that different ethnic groups count differently; for some first generation means the first to immigrate here, for others, it's the first generation born here. When in doubt, ask.

- *Why their forebears came to America,* that is, career advancement, better educational opportunities for their children, refugee resettlement, politically-driven circumstances. This "story" may be the most important to hear. We can't truly know someone until we are aware of the most significant events of their past and how they impact who they are today.

- *Acumen of their mother tongue.* Is it their first or second language? Which language is spoken at home? Most first- and some second-generation Asian Americans are self-conscious about their English language skills. Genuine, sensitive affirmation (versus "Gee, you speak good English!") goes a long way.

- *Where the first generation settled and what their experiences were like in that community.* Were they accepted? Were they discriminated against? Did they live in an enclave or community with others of the same nationality or did they work hard to assimilate?

- *Occupations they entered.* Was it their occupation in the homeland or were they forced to give that up and find a different line of work?

- *Their personal encounters with prejudice and racism.* Everyone responds differently. The same episode may evoke night-and-day different reactions from two individuals. From one, a laugh and a shrug; from another, angry eyes and scathing indictments.

- *Feelings about other ethnic groups.* How does your nationality tend to feel about other Asian Americans? African Americans? Hispanic Americans? Caucasians? Do you share those feelings?

- *Expectations placed on them by their parents* in areas like career, marriage choices, where they will live after college graduation, the role they are expected to play when their parents retire. For a lengthy, in-depth understanding of this, see *Following Jesus Without Dishonoring Your Parents.*

In addition, I find it helpful to ask some specific, nationality-related questions. Here are a few:

- *Korean Americans:* How do you feel about Japanese Americans given the things done to Koreans by the Japanese in the twentieth century, like the Korean comfort women? Does it affect your own relationships with Japanese Americans, especially Japanese American men?

- *Japanese Americans:* Did you have relatives who were sent to internment camps during World War II? Which camp or camps were they in and what was their experience like there? How did it affect their attitudes about the United States government? Toward Caucasians? Are they still bitter?

- *Chinese Americans from Taiwan:* Do you consider yourself primarily Taiwanese American or Chinese American? Why? How do you feel toward the other?

- *Chinese Americans:* How do you feel about Japanese Americans given the things done to the Chinese by the Japanese in the first half of the twentieth century, like the "Rape of Nanking"?

- *Vietnamese Americans:* What were the circumstances involved in your coming to the United States? What did your family lose or leave behind in Vietnam? Was your family put in refugee camps? What was your experience like?

- *Filipino Americans:* Filipino Americans have been called an invisible minority. In what areas have your family and Filipino American friends been discriminated against due to lack of political representation? What do you feel you have in common with other Asian Americans? In what ways do you feel disconnected from other Asian Americans?

- *South Asian Americans:* How do feel about the tensions between Pakistan and India? How do Pakistani Americans and Indian Americans relate to each other? How closely do you identify with other Asian Americans? What can other Asian Americans do to make you feel more at home at Asian American gatherings? Are there other ethnicities you relate to more easily than Asian Americans?

- *Biracial and multiracial Asian Americans:* (Recognize this may be awkward to discuss.) What ethnicities make up your cultural heritage? What things do you like about each ethnicity? What things do you dislike or have a hard time with? Do you identify with both sides of your ethnicity or do you tend to lean toward one over the other? Why do you think you do that?

Is there anything in the histories of each ethnicity that informs your leanings? Do you ever feel shame being one or the other? Does being biracial create a deeper richness in your life or confusion or angst? Do you feel you get the benefits of two cultures or do you feel robbed of being fully of one?

Asking such questions helps me to not generalize. I already own too long a list of Asian American faux pas:

- I assumed Brian *Chang* and Helen *Lee* were Chinese American and not Korean American.

- When assembling an address list of InterVarsity's Asian American staff, I left off a Thai American because *Balasiri* didn't "sound" Asian to me.

- I assumed a biracial Asian American valued the Asian side about fifty percent less than I did.

I could go on.

DIFFERENT, SOMETIMES WAY DIFFERENT

Diverse and becoming more diverse aptly describes current Asian America. According to the fine print in the 2000 census, there are thirty-two different Asian American and thirty-four different Native Hawaiian and Pacific Islander nationalities. We are not a monolithic culture. We are at very different places in our assimilation into American culture and in developing our ethnic identity.

My grandparents came to California at the start of the twentieth century. Our fourth generation biracial son Sam has a close Hmong American friend whose family was in refugee camps in Thailand starting in 1975. His parents speak very little English and are raising a toddler to speak Hmong as her first language. Those are big differences in our backgrounds and heritage.

Even within nationalities, the differences can be huge. What the Ph.D. student with roots in Beijing encounters at a midwestern university is distinctly different from the world of the dishwasher immigrating from Guandong to New York City. They're both Chinese Americans but very different in background, culture, education, aspirations and what they'll eat for dinner tonight.

Using ethnic identity and assimilation as constructs, Asian Americans will generally fall into four categories. *Assimilation* includes integration into schools, work places and social groupings of the majority culture, identification with the majority culture and marrying someone from the majority culture. *Ethnic identity* focuses on the retention of ethnic ways.

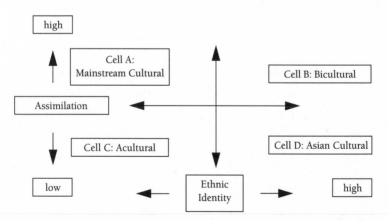

Figure 12.1. Ethnic identity/assimilation grid

The ethnic identity/assimilation grid in figure 12.1 comes from the work of Harry Kitano and Roger Daniels.[1] The following applications and observations have been supplied by Asian American church and parachurch leader Jeanette Yep with some additional input from Greg Jao and myself.

Cell A—high assimilation, low ethnic identity

- see themselves as more American than Asian
- feel completely at home in the dominant culture
- are assimilated and accepted
- feel as out-of-place in a large gathering of Asian Americans as many non-Asians do
- have little interest in exploring their Asian identity, language, culture
- are usually third and succeeding generations of Asian Americans and may have grown up isolated from other Asians
- relate to a high number of non-Asians in their friendship and social patterns
- have a high rate of outmarriage

Cell B—high assimilation, high ethnic identity

- can be/feel as assimilated as a Cell A person but retain a strong sense of Asian identity
- reflect a bicultural perspective in their friendship patterns, membership in organizations and so on
- move back and forth between American and Asian cultures easily
- are interested in keeping their ethnic heritage alive and are quite knowledgeable about it
- can serve as bridge people between cultures

Cell C—low assimilation, low ethnic identity

- have acquired little American culture and are also uncomfortable with an ethnic identity

- can feel estranged, disenchanted and disillusioned
- aren't at home in either of the two cultures they find themselves in
- may include some first generation Eurasians and some biracial people
- include some Vietnamese and Hmong refugees
- may have had bad immigration experiences and haven't assimilated

Cell D—low assimilation, high ethnic identity
- can include newly arrived immigrants (especially of advanced age)
- identify more closely to the ethnic community than the American one
- tend to live with fellow Cell D types
- may include Asian Americans who feel white society will never treat them as equals
- are very unlikely to marry non-Asian Americans
- are culturally more ethnic than American

Within each of these four "types" of Asian Americans is still more diversity. Not every Cell D Asian American walks, talks and acts alike. Case in point: Cell D Pakistani Americans and Korean Americans, while both caring deeply about their ethnic identity, will rarely find themselves in the same social or religious settings. Within each quadrant is a lot of range and variety.

To make ministry to Asian Americans all the more complex and intriguing, it is done in the context of an increasingly multiethnic nation. Kitano and Daniel's chart must be seen as one side of a three-dimensional cube. The biblical call is and has always been to be more than monocultural. The future kingdom of God is multiethnic (Rev 7:9) and part of our mission now is to work out Jesus' model prayer, "Your kingdom come, your will be done on earth as it is in heaven" (Mt 6:10).

As we seek to live out that prayer, we might find it actually easier for those of us Cell B type Asian Americans to relate to Cell B types of *non-Asian cultures and heritages* than it is for us to relate to Cell A, C and D

Asian Americans. Perhaps it will be the Cell B's of the different ethnicities who are the vanguard of authentic multiethnic ministry.

When working with Asian Americans, it helps to know where they are in the development of their ethnic identity and how assimilated into American culture they are. It will greatly impact how you choose to develop them as leaders.

I recently consulted with the young adult fellowship leadership team of a Chinese American church. I introduced the chart above then asked, "Where do the young adults in your fellowship fall? What quadrant are they in?"

A lively discussion ensued with the following conclusion: "We are B's and we attract mostly A's who want to become B's."

When I asked what they meant by this, they said that growing up as second generation Chinese Americans, they felt the need to fit in and be accepted by their white peers (high assimilation). In grade school and high school especially, no one liked to stick out and be "weird." While they might "be Chinese" on Sundays, going to Chinese church and taking Chinese language lessons, the other six days demanded "whiteness" to survive.

When they reached college, multiculturalism was structurally affirmed and minorities were usually in greater number than in their high schools. So they experienced more freedom to figure out what the Chinese of "Chinese American" meant. Now as young adults, most of them away from home, many contemplating marriage, the desire increased to take their "Asian-ness" seriously (high ethnic identity).

While some of their Chinese American friends from college opted for majority culture churches, they intentionally chose a Chinese church because they wanted their ethnicity affirmed and nurtured. Another reason behind their choice was that many wanted to marry another Chinese American.

Most college age and young adult Asian Americans who are at least second generation would be in the first two categories in the Kitano and Daniels framework—highly assimilated with either low or high ethnic identity. College students who have low ethnic identity usually will feel most comfortable in multiethnic or predominantly white campus organizations. Those with high ethnic identity will choose groups that attract mostly Asian Americans. The same general pattern holds true for churches.

OUTREACHING THE UNREACHED PLANET: UNCHURCHED ASIAN AMERICANS

- They're reading *Giant Robot* and *AsianWeek*.
- They're part Japanese, part something else.
- They're activists; look for them in the campus APA groups and grass-roots community organizations.
- They're dot-commers.
- They're driving rice rockets.
- They may not answer to Asian American.
- They're gay/lesbian.
- Their leadership training comes from LEAP or their MBA program, not from the church.
- They care deeply about their families.
- They're Buddhist, trying to figure out what that means.
- They're our brother, sister, mother, father.
- They're working on their golf stroke on Sunday mornings.
- Their hair was at one time black.
- They think Christianity is . . . stop . . . they don't think about Christianity.
- They're at Harvard.
- They're not in college.
- They love "Iron Chef."

Who are they? *Unchurched Asian Americans*: second to sixth generation Asian Americans untouched, unfound, unloved by the church.

They are everywhere but because most of our time is spent with people a lot like us, they are usually invisible to us. We don't see them because we choose not to. We don't even wish they would go away because they make us feel uncomfortable; in our world, they don't exist. Except for those in our nuclear family, they never even hit our radar screen. We can coexist merrily as separate planets. The *social insulation* between us is at least R-30 in thickness.

Missiologists would call them an "unreached people group," those nobody is connecting with on a spiritual level.

How will Jesus reach them? Probably through people who dwell in their world, do what they do and think in similar ways. Does that exclude us? It doesn't have to. Most of us spend enormous relational energy finding people who are as much like us as possible. We don't realize our common culture provides more of a bridge to unchurched Asian Americans than we might think. We should not underrate our cultural connection.

CASE STUDY: REACHING COLLEGE STUDENTS

The leaders of the Northwestern University Asian American Christian Ministry made a decision at their annual leadership camp that impacted everything they did the following year. Their staff worker, Kathy Khang, told them, "We always talk a good game about caring about the lost, then we go right on programming everything for Christians." She challenged them to "act like we really do care." She had grown tired of the fellowship of just being a safe place for churched Asian Americans who were looking for something that reminded them of their youth groups back home.

For the entire year, every weekly fellowship meeting was designed for seekers—the theme for the year, the music, the dramas, the message, the types of prayers, everything. The fellowship lost some members when they announced their bold plan. But seekers started coming in significant numbers. At times it was awkward for the fellowship but the awkwardness took a back seat when some of the seekers came to faith in Jesus. The following year the theme of outreach continued to be center stage. What was once a haven for Christians became a lighthouse for the spiritually lost.

Strategically, college is probably the most opportune time to connect with secular Asian Americans. On campus, where a student's world is smaller and more self-contained, opportunities abound. Asian American cultural and social organizations can be found on most campuses.

Marie Ting, who served as program coordinator in the Office of Academic Multicultural Initiatives at the University of Michigan, told me about an Asian American believer who intentionally chose involvement in the United Asian American Organizations, the central organization for all Asian American students. He joined in order to "mix it up" with more nonbelievers. When the UM Chinese Christian Fellowship sponsored an outreach coffeehouse, he invited his UAAO friends. Because they had grown to enjoy and respect him, over a dozen of his new friends came.

Involvement with organizations like the JACL, OCA or Asian-oriented cultural events provide the few post-college opportunities to meet and befriend Asian American nonbelievers.

Some things needed for reaching the unchurched:

- *A passion for the unchurched.* The apostle Paul captures well his passion for "his" people in Romans 9:1-4: "I speak the truth in Christ—I am not lying, my conscience confirms it in the Holy Spirit—I have great sorrow and unceasing anguish in my heart. For I could wish that I myself were cursed and cut off from Christ for the sake of my brothers, those of my own race, the people of Israel." We need leaders who feel likewise for the unchurched.

- *The ability to color outside the lines.* Adding drums to worship services and watching *The Fast and the Furious* twice won't be enough. Getting and keeping the attention of unchurched Asian Americans will take leaders not bound to traditional forms of outreach, worship, preaching, discipleship, prayer, celebrations and partying. How will you find these leaders? Start by looking for those who like to spend their free time with the unchurched.

- *The blessing of church and fellowship leaders.* When I served as the president of our campus fellowship my junior year, I sensed God was pulling me to another arena of leadership. Taking a deep breath, I told our leadership team I felt God wanting me to run for student body president. Instead of reacting, "Secular leadership—what for?" they released me from my fellowship responsibilities so I could devote all my energies to campaigning. Just as important, they give me their full blessing.

I couldn't have run wholeheartedly without it. Likewise, we may need to release and bless some of our leaders for ministry on this unreached planet.

- *Resources.* It will certainly cost money, even reallocating funds. Some longstanding programs may need to cease in order to provide financial resources for outreach.

- *Prayer.* When things aren't working, when great ideas don't come, when people quit, when discouragement is pervasive, when criticism feels unbearable, knowing they are undergirded by the prayers of others will help get them through awful times.

- *The freedom to experiment wildly and fail big-time.* President Franklin Roosevelt's advice: "But above all, try something." An executive at Cadbury offers this: "Ready. Fire. Aim." Missiologist Ralph Winter: "I am willing to fail. Risks are not to be evaluated in terms of the probability of success but in terms of the value of goal."

13

TELLING THE TRUTH ABOUT ASIAN AMERICAN SECRETS

J unior year I lived with three guys. We were all quite busy with academics, fellowship responsibilities and the like, but we tried to make Sunday night our "family time." It was our scheduled time to check in with each other to see how we were doing as individuals and as a household. Sometimes there was little to report on, other times we went for hours. Occasionally, when designated chores went undone (nothing nastier than a bathroom shared by four single guys!) or we got on each other's nerves, candor and grace were called upon.

Similarly, within the Asian American church family, we sometimes have *our issues*. Pull up a chair and have a seat so we can discuss a few pressing matters. It's hard for anyone to do this. It doesn't help that our "Asian DNA" includes conflict-avoidance genes that elevate peacekeeping above truth telling about ourselves. This chapter is our family time. We have the following matters to discuss:

- Our world needs to include more than our own.

- Current church leaders must pass the baton of leadership to the next generation.

- We need to treat gifted women leaders fairly.

- We must stop the "silent exodus" of young Asian Americans from the church.

GOING BEYOND "OUR OWN":
BECOMING AN ASIAN AMERICAN OR MULTIETHNIC BODY

It's bigger than us.

My family and I are active in Atlanta Chinese Christian Church. The church began in the late 1960s as a Bible study for Georgia Tech graduate students from Taiwan. Those who chose to remain in Atlanta and stay with the Bible study helped it grow into a church. When services were first held, they were in Mandarin. Later, as they had children, an English service was formed.

We started attending in 1995. In 2002, the church numbered about 900. I am the only Japanese American; Margaret, one of two Caucasian American females; Sam, the only biracial Japanese-Caucasian. Our involvement has been warmly welcomed and encouraged by church leaders and members.

I've watched—with personal interest at stake—as other non-Chinese Americans have shown up. Would other interracial couples be welcomed, even when one spouse is African American? Recently a young Caucasian American man was baptized—who was he?

In the past few years, our English congregation leaders have initiated fellowship opportunities with other Asian American churches in metro Atlanta. Our English congregation pastor is white and our worship leader is Korean American. The main speakers at our major youth conference the past few years have been African American and Vietnamese American.

From my vantage point, ACCC gets an A for effort. In fact, part of its original vision when chartered as a church in 1977 was to reach out beyond Chinese Americans. Our registered name is "Atlanta Christian Fellowship, Inc." The intent was always to be open to be broader than a Chinese American church.

A huge decision facing our church's leadership will be: "Should ACCC become a multiethnic or pan-Asian church or should we remain Atlanta *Chinese* Christian Church?" On the surface, the question appears straightforward. But more difficult questions lie below the surface.

If we strive to become truly multiethnic, it means we will be a church for any ethnicity to attend. Our youth will be affirmed as they invite their non-Chinese friends to attend youth group activities. But how will we feel if one of "our own" starts dating a non-Chinese American, especially a non-Asian American? How will we feel if ACCC becomes known throughout Atlanta as the premier church where interracial couples are welcomed? What will we do if some of them are African American-Asian American couples?

Thus far ACCC appears to be batting a perfect 1.000. Three "tests" came recently when favorite daughters of the church respectively married a Caucasian, an Indian American and a Korean American. I've not heard one negative comment about any of these relationships.

If we choose to become a truly multiethnic congregation, will we welcome the neighbors to attend, even as the neighborhood turns Hispanic? How will we change our worship services and other activities to be more Hispanic-friendly? Will we offer Spanish language lessons in addition to our Sunday afternoon Chinese language school?

We have had an outreach to the Vietnamese American community for nearly ten years. About five miles from the church is Woodgate, a large apartment complex where numerous Vietnamese families have settled. We have ministered effectively to them at the complex but rarely have the families visited the church. If we became a pan-Asian church, how would we feel about embracing these Vietnamese families? Are we comfortable with their youth socializing with our youth as peers and not just as part of our outreach?

On one level are ethnicity differences. On another level that is perhaps even more significant are socioeconomic issues. ACCC is an upper middle class church with a high percentage of white-collar professionals. We aren't as good at being a comfortable church home for those less educated or in blue-collar professions.

It wouldn't stop there, if we choose to be truly multiethnic. Historically in Atlanta there have been white churches and black churches (and a small sprinkling of "other churches"). An invisible horizontal "Mason-Dixon Line" divides Atlanta's white and black populations. Whites, in general, have lived north of the line, and African Americans, in general, south of it. As blacks have prospered and developed into the largest African American middle class in the country, the line has risen northward as their buying power has increased. As this has occurred, the white population (in order to not live among and have their children go to school with blacks) has moved farther north where land is available and affordable. With this the invisible line has risen northward.

Right now that line is just about where our church is located. Will we go the way of many white churches and relocate? Or will we be open to another ethnic minority group—even though our differences tend to eclipse our camaraderie as minorities? Again ACCC has done some good things, welcoming its few African American visitors and occasionally bringing in African American speakers.

Two years ago we started a second congregation in one of the far north suburbs of Atlanta. As the demographics keep changing around our mother church, it could be "convenient" for our members to start attending ACCC-North. In a matter of five to ten years, we could have role reversal— we becoming the smaller daughter church of the growing northern congregation. If we did so, we would be following the traditional pattern of white churches in Atlanta. When members will be asked, "Why did you switch churches?" we can give the time-honored answer, "We just feel more comfortable at the northern church." May that not happen.

Evergreen Baptist Church of Los Angeles is a church that has embraced the diversity of their city. Pastor Ken Fong leads the congregation with a deep commitment to broadening the landscape. What began as an *Issei* (first generation Japanese American) church in 1925 branched into two Asian American churches in 1997.

One of them, the church Fong pastors, had a vision "to become something I never used to think was preferable or possible: a multi-Asian/multiethnic, multi-socioeconomic, multigenerational congregation."[1] The church currently encompasses more then ten Asian Pacific American groups, spans five generations and is becoming intentionally more multiethnic.

If Asian nationality-specific churches around the country intentionally choose to become pan-Asian American (perhaps on their way to becoming authentically multiethnic), difficult questions will need to be faced and answered honestly.

One set of questions must deal with forgiveness of past things:

- Can Korean Americans offer "generational forgiveness" to Japanese Americans for the atrocities of the Japanese military on their "comfort women?"

- Can Chinese Americans offer similar forgiveness for the "Rape of Nanking"?

- Can Japanese American forgive Caucasians and the U.S. government for the internment of 120,000 ancestors during World War II?

- Can Korean Americans let go of any animosity they feel toward African Americans for the looting and burning of scores of Korean-owned stores during the 1992 Los Angeles riots?

If forgiveness for specific sins of the past isn't sought, authentic fellowship won't happen; there will always be giant, invisible elephants in the room that no one discusses but all know are there.

Next to put on the table are the hard questions dealing with multiethnic or pan-Asian congregational life. They need to include:

- "Will I stay if my ethnic group, now in the majority, becomes the minority?"

- "Am I comfortable having leaders—pastors, elders and deacons, especially—who are of the nationalities represented in our congregation?"

- "Am I willing to have the church located where it is accessible to our target audience, even if I'm not very comfortable with the neighborhood around it?"

Here's the potential deal-breaker, the price too high for most churches to pay:

- "Will I allow my daughter or son to marry a _____?"

If the answer is no, the level of authentic koinonia (fellowship) will plateau at a low-risk level. On this issue I have watched the most open and deeply committed believers draw their line in the sand and quietly step to the "no" side.

I'm reminded of the wealthy leader who found eternal life an attractive proposition. When Jesus told him it would cost him that which was dear to him—his homes, lifestyle and investments—he counted the cost and "became very sad" (Lk 18:22). The true wealth of many Asian Americans is having their children investing in the things they themselves hold dear—a marriage partner of the same nationality being one of them.

Prior to our involvement in ACCC, we were active in a church that found the demographics of its surrounding suburban Atlanta neighborhood rapidly changing. When the church began in the mid-1970s, the area was predominantly white and middle class. About twenty years later, it became predominantly black and middle class.

In 1992 I was asked to lead a Sunday school class on developing into a multiethnic church. I declined but said I would like to lead one on what I thought was the real question members and visitors were asking, "Should Our Church Become a Black and White Church?" I was the only Asian American in the church, but I knew that was clearly the issue we were all thinking about.

For twelve weeks we met and discussed topics like "Understanding Atlanta's Changing Racial Demographics" (subtitled "Why Is Your House Really Up for Sale?"), "A Short Course in Black History," and "The Benefits and Costs of Reaching Our Neighborhood." The class packed out and discussions were lively, animated and often quite impassioned. Every Sunday afternoon I had to take a nap. The class wreaked havoc on my Asian peacemaking genes and left me exhausted.

My best friend in the church, a Caucasian elder, asked to have lunch with me during the middle of the series. He chewed me out for bringing in "that angry black man" to teach a unit on "Why African Americans and Whites Don't Get Along That Well" (subtitled "The Gospel According to Spike Lee"). For two hours over lunch, we yelled back and forth at each other. Losing his friendship was painful but the class was invaluable to many. It gave us a place to express what before we were only allowed to feel and verbalize in whispers to confidantes.

It was the best Sunday school class I've ever participated in. Not because I led it, but because it was *not* a class where everyone nodded in unison with the teacher.

At its conclusion, I wrote a summary recommendation to the leadership board that I didn't think we should become a black and white church. As stretching as the class was for all of us, I felt like we wouldn't be able to pay the cost. I feared that we would begin strong, welcoming African Americans to join us, but when the "honeymoon" period ended, it would be too hard for us and we would move on to something a little less challenging. Who would be left out on the limb? The African Americans who took the risk to join us. That was too costly a price to pay.

Some ten years later, I'm happily proven wrong. The church is working extremely hard at being a neighborhood church. It refuses to move to Atlanta's far exurbs. They have an outstanding African American pastor. They are the only evangelical church I'm aware of in Atlanta trying to be a black and white church, and for the most part, they are succeeding.

How has it been for the white members who stayed? To a one, I believe they would say, "Hard and rich, hard and rich." I admire them so much.

IF IT'S A RELAY, WHO HAS THE BATON?

The second challenge is for *immigrant church leaders to pass the baton of leadership to the next generation.*

I was speaking at a college weekend conference for a Korean American church in the Northeast. I met several young adults who loved the church but were getting increasingly frustrated. They respected their elders but at the same time felt they could make significant contributions in leading the church. They weren't being asked.

"Paul, would you sit in on a meeting we're having with several of the elders?" they asked me. "Maybe you can help us hear each other out." There was desperation in their voices. As we met for lunch that Sunday over some great bulgogi and bi bim bop, the young adults expressed their respect for the elders and their love of the church. Then they tentatively mentioned their openness to taking on more leadership and asked why they weren't being taken up on their offers.

The elders said they had offered such opportunities, but when they weren't handled well, they recalled the offer.

What makes it so hard for the immigrant church leaders to firmly place the leadership baton into the hands of the next generation—and let go?

"In Asian culture, you have a very slow giving over of authority and control to the younger generation," says Robert Goette, director of Asian American Church Consulting in Chicago. "Often, the control resides with the parents until they die."[2]

As much as the parent (the older generation that built the church) loves the child (the next generation), it is usually very hard for them to let go and allow them to "grow up" and assume responsibility for some of their own decisions. If the older generation *founded* the church, it is all the harder for them to let go of their "baby."

The dilemma demands cooperation from both sides. The next generation can do things that say "You can trust us" to the elders. They can seek to live out 1 Corinthians 13:4-7 in their relationships with their elders, being patient when change is slow in coming, showing kindness, not envying what the elders have, not boasting about their own capabilities nor being proud of them, not seeking position or power for selfish reasons and not having a short fuse when change isn't forthcoming at a reasonable speed.

Perhaps the hardest part of the passage for the emerging leaders to live out is keeping no record of wrongs when they want to angrily wave a laundry list of times they've been misunderstood or treated poorly. Find ways in which you can help them live by this credo (my application of 1 Corinthians 13:7):

- We will always protect our elders.
- We will always trust our elders.
- We will always hope the best for our elders.
- We will always persevere with our elders.

The elders likewise need to apply this passage in their relationships with the emerging generation.

As a "leader of emerging leaders," you can help them put themselves in the shoes of their elders so they can understand their perspective on the church. The movie *The Divine Secrets of the Ya-Ya Sisterhood* tells the story of a mother and her thirtysomething daughter tangling and trying to make sense of their complex relationship. It takes the mother's "ya-ya sisters," her lifelong friends, to intervene and help the daughter understand some past events that made her mother the way she is.

Asian American churches—especially those serving the first and second generations because there are dramatic differences in these two generations—need "ya-ya" sisters and (yo-yo?) brothers to help the younger generation understand their elders' behavior. Help them by urging them to pray for their elders, to not gossip (to say nothing behind someone's back that they would not say directly to them) and build trust and respect from the elders by excelling in whatever they're asked to do. Encourage them to put service over positions and titles.

ADVOCATING FOR WOMEN LEADERS

The third challenge facing us is *treating gifted women leaders fairly.* One of the loneliest places in Christendom is where a gifted woman is not allowed to use her gifts in ministry. How much richer and more enjoyable the kingdom of God would be if women were allowed to lead in the same ways men are!

While it is my theological conviction that women should be given the same opportunities for ministry as men, I affirm those who arrive at different conclusions *after* their study of Scripture has likewise led them there. It is critical—whatever position we take—that we not arrive at it via tradition ("it's what my church has always taught"), comfortability ("I'd rather not challenge the status quo and risk conflict") or sloppy exegesis ("these two verses seem pretty plain to me, so that settles it").

Churches can easily fall prey to any of these three pitfalls. As new Asian American churches are planted, it is imperative that the pioneering leaders—both men and women alike—study the Scriptures collectively and prayerfully to arrive at their conclusions. Most Asian American churches do not give women the same opportunities for ministry as men. Once things are done a certain way for two or three generations, the concrete is set.

Often a young woman who has been active leader in a campus fellow-ship graduates and looks for a church where her leadership gifts can be utilized. She may have even led her fellowship on campus with responsi-bilities for several hundred students, but the most she is offered at the church is to teach preschoolers. When word gets around that "sister" has something good to say, she is often asked to "share" away from the pulpit and led to the nearest music stand. Frustration sets in.

When Asian American church leaders fret about their young adults leaving, it would help them to ask, "What do we let women do here?" fol-lowed by "Why don't we let them do more?"

Men in leadership, don't let your sisters get buffeted and beat up all alone. Advocate and promote them.

THE "SILENT EXODUS" OF YOUNG ASIAN AMERICANS FROM THE CHURCH

A fourth challenge we face is figuring out *how to minister to those who have left the church.*

"The surge in Asian immigration led to an explosion of new churches," wrote Helen Lee in the mid-1990s. "But the flip side of the success story has been a silent exodus of church-raised young people who find their im-migrant churches irrelevant, culturally stifling, and ill-equipped to devel-op them spiritually for life in the multicultural 1990s. Of those young people who have left their parents' churches, few have chosen to attend non-Asian churches."[3]

That exodus continues into the twenty-first century. Allen Thompson, coordinator for multicultural church planning in the Presbyterian Church of America, says, "The second generation is being lost. They are the mission field we need to focus on."

Samuel Ling, president of China Horizon and author of *The "Chinese" Way of Doing Things,* estimates only about four percent of American Born Chinese (ABCs), who constitute 40 percent of the U.S. Chinese popula-tion, are integrated into the Chinese church.[4]

"Some 70 percent of first-generation Korean Americans are affiliated with a Korean church in the U.S. today," wrote Lee, but most 1.5 (those born in Korea and moved to the United States as a child) and second generation Korean Americans strongly prefer a church where English—not Korean—is the primary language.[5]

Daniel Lee, a first-generation pastor at Global Mission Church in Silver Spring, Maryland, says, "The Korean church in America, in general, is very busy just trying to survive. It hasn't had enough energy or time to focus on the second generation yet."[6]

Japanese Americans are the most assimilated of all Asian American nationalities and have the highest rate of marrying out of any ethnic minority. Timothy Tseng, church history professor at American Baptist Seminary of the West, says, "I don't see too many new Japanese-only churches forming unless the younger generations start them—which I doubt they will."[7]

All to say this: a whole lot of Asian American young people with some grasp of biblical truth might be evangelized or "re-evangelized" as the case may be. Clearly, if they are to be reached, it will have to be with new wineskins. What we invite them to *become* must be an authentic biblical image of a new creation. What we invite them to *become a part of* must connect well with at least these parts of their being: Asian, American, what stage in life they are in (i.e., college student, young adult, middle aged adult, beyond) and their spiritual hunger.

In a 1999 interview for *re:generation quarterly* David Gibbons, pastor of NewSong Community Church in Irvine, California, says:

> There is an emerging group of people who want to reach what has been called the "silent exodus" of Asian Americans. Iwa, a ministry here in California, has determined that 97 percent of Asian Americans leave their church after college. The ethnic churches may boast about enormous youth or college ministries, but once their children graduate from college, they're gone. Our hope [at NewSong] is to be part of bringing this silent exodus— the misfits, the prodigals, the artists, and the marginalized—back to God. In a word, our mission is reconciliation.[8]

Gibbons is not calling for dissolving first generation churches. "Before planting [NewSong]," Helen Lee says, "Gibbons obtained the blessing of first-generation church leaders, explaining he was not trying to steal their young people but was partnering with them to reach unchurched Asian Americans."[9]

Likewise, I want to affirm the immigrant church. I can vouch for its considerable merit. With continued immigration from Asia, the need for such churches will remain, but the breadth of their ministry is limited. We need more churches and ministries targeting those who have left the church.

STOPPING THE "SILENT EXODUS"

What can we do to minister well to those who have left the church?

Plant Asian American churches. Rare is the immigrant church that has become or has birthed an authentically Asian American church that has lasted. The better strategy seems to be akin to Gibbons's: obtain the blessing and perhaps sponsorship of the immigrant churches to reach the immigrants' children and grandchildren.

Pan-Asian churches are a big piece of the future for reaching and keeping second- to sixth-generation Asian Americans. Most major Asian American hubs are able to sustain at least one Asian American church.

In California and New York City, there is room and need for several. They'll work in California because Asian Americans span several generations and at least the East Asian Americans mix well. New York is unique because people have been forced to live and cope in close proximity, and the city attracts almost every nationality imaginable. Both states for the most part possess progressive attitudes toward race.

Denominations like the Evangelical Covenant and American Baptist Churches have been forward-thinking in sponsoring pan-Asian American churches.

Don't be afraid to form informal limited alliances with secular Asian American groups with whom your church or fellowship share some common values. In almost every major city, there are chapters of the JACL and the OCA and other Asian American civic-oriented groups. There are also groups for Asian American business professionals, manufacturers, lawyers, media and the like. (Did you know about the Association of Chinese-American Engineers and Scientists of New Mexico?)

On most medium to large college and university campuses, there are at least a handful of Asian American clubs. Student activities offices keep lists of all campus organizations.

As a senior at Cal Poly, I joined Tomo Dachi Kai, the Japanese student club. I didn't have the nerve to go alone, so I coerced Andy Mori, the only other Japanese American in our Christian fellowship, to join with me. I can't say I was always comfortable there; it was the first all-Asian group I had belonged to since leaving the Buddhist church in high school.

When Andy and I would informally debrief ("What did they mean by that?") we'd often mention a "cultural connection" we experienced and we didn't have in our almost all-white fellowship.

Most of us won't experience a "hand in glove" fit when involved in these cultural organizations. I usually don't. Politically, they may be at a different place than we are. We may disagree with their reasons and motives on various issues. The national organization may take stands we can't endorse. Each believer must determine how compatible their views must be with organizations in which they choose to be involved. I've chosen to be involved in the local JACL because it's been a way for me to be tied into and give back a little to my ethnic community. It's a place where I can be salt and light. I've also had opportunities to share my faith with individual members after gaining their trust and respect.

Promote nonconfrontational group-oriented evangelism. Pastor Ken Fong writes, "Many times, unconvinced Americanized Asian Americans will secretly resent the person posing such a direct challenge to them, for in most Asian cultures, direct confrontation is to be avoided at all costs because of the inherent risk of unnecessarily obligating someone and/or causing another to lose face. Those are grave social errors."[10]

For Asian Americans, evangelism or outreach begins with the group, not the individual. Group activities lead to personal conversations somewhere down the road, if it's appropriate and comfortable.

A hallmark of almost every Asian American fellowship I've interacted with is they are flat-out fun, enjoyable people to be around. Their winsomeness and zest for life is a magnet that draws others into the life of their fellowship.

The Asian American Christian Fellowship at Boston University in the late 1990s was one of my favorite groups to visit. They were welcoming, hospitable, fun-loving, loving, at times goofy. As I watched them relate to other students in the student union and dining hall, I pictured myself as a nonbeliever at BU. *I'd want to hang with these folks! Whatever they have is worth checking out.*

Another favorite group is Northwestern University's Asian Christian Ministry. I attended one of their meetings aimed at Asian American nonbelievers. They had a time of seeker-sensitive worship and a drama geared to them, not the Christians. They asked me to speak directly to nonbelievers, as if the Christians weren't even there. After the meeting, folk hung around for at least an hour—on a Friday night!

The next morning, I led an Asian American leadership seminar for Chicago students. Kathy Khang, the staff worker, told me that they had invited the whole fellowship to come, including non-Christians and several showed up.

As a fellowship, they started GIGs (Groups Investigating God), small groups designed to introduce students to the Jesus of the Bible. They were a natural follow-up to the other outreach-oriented activities they had.

On most campuses where there is a sizeable Asian American population, there will always be some who want to hang with other Asian Americans. Our Asian American fellowships can provide an oasis for them.

Foster collaborative leadership, not lordship leadership. For many young Asian Americans brought up in a first- or second-generation church, the leadership model was often an authoritarian-oriented "leader as lord." This is especially true for Korean Americans, less so for Japanese Americans with other Asian Americans somewhere in-between.

Young leaders prefer to be on "servant teams." Being the president of a fellowship appeals to few. Group-based leadership feels more authentic and more in sync with their relational culture.

A collaborative style of leadership will especially appeal to women. Jung Ha Kim writes in her chapter, "The Labor of Compassion: Voices of Churched Korean American Women" in *New Spiritual Homes: Religion and Asian Americans*:

In the context of this deeply gendered and highly ethnicity-conscious institution, churched Korean American women recognize that their own church relegates them to secondary status and systematically excludes them from gaining public recognition. They are also aware that much of the church work is done by women, yet male church leaders tend to get the credit.[11]

Offer mentoring by "elders" and accountability within a shame-based culture. Almost ten years ago, I was asked to speak at a conference for students from UCLA and Occidental College. I was told ahead of time there would be "a good many" Asian American students present.

As we were getting ready to hop on the ferry that took us from Long Beach to Catalina Island, Doug Schaupp, the conference director, pulled me aside. "Paul, a lot of the Asian Americans—especially the guys—are really looking forward to being around you." He explained why. "They don't have many older role models who look like them."

I thought it was a nice thing for Doug to say to make me feel comfortable. When Sunday afternoon arrived and I slowly (read: exhausted) got off the ferry in Long Beach, I realized I never had more than a ten-minute break. When I wasn't speaking, I had wall-to-wall appointments with students, many of them Asian American men. Perhaps the most helpful thing I gave them was the hope that an Asian American man could be over forty and still love Jesus.

When I returned to my "day job" as Southeastern regional director for InterVarsity, I recalled a story I had heard at a previous Urbana missions convention. The speaker was talking about the need for missionaries in places like Afghanistan. He said something like, "If you see ten people in a river pushing a log on one end and one person pushing the other end, which end are you going to help?"

I realized there were probably more people who could take my job in the Southeast than there were older Asian American men to be a mentor for younger Asian American men. A few years later, I became InterVarsity's Asian American ministry coordinator and have loved almost every minute of it.

Worship Asian American style. Worship that connects with the heart and mind is not icing on the cake for this generation. For some, it is the cake. James Choung, a seasoned worship leader in San Diego, points to four unique qualities that need to be present in Asian American worship: freedom, authenticity, intimacy and intensity.

Freedom. The deepest place of worship for Asian Americans is where we can be ourselves. In our culture, we find ourselves restrained from our true desires and feelings, deferring often to our elders or our community. Asian Americans treasure a worship setting that provides freedom. The sense of freedom often occurs when three other values are embraced: authenticity, intimacy and intensity.

Authenticity. The Asian American worshiper needs to have a sense of authenticity. Not only do they need to feel as if the worship leader is fully authentic and engaged in worship, they themselves also need to feel authentic when singing the truths written in these songs. No songs are sung that cannot be done so with integrity. A minister once wryly quipped, "Christians don't say lies, they sing 'em." Asian Americans don't want to sing something they cannot fully believe and thus fully engage.

Intimacy. For Asian Americans, worship is not merely having fun with quick-paced songs. Its strength is not in celebration (as in the black church or Latino church) nor solid theology (as in more traditional white churches) nor merely solid musicianship (as in more contemporary white churches). Bringing a sense of intimacy with God is vital.

Asian American worship leaders often speak much less (as in an Asian family), allowing the nonverbal aspects of worship to minister. Not all the worship songs need to be explained as is often done in white settings, nor do Asian Americans want to be told what to do as is done frequently in black settings.

What Asian Americans want is to find freedom through intimacy. Slower, more meditative songs during a worship set—along with the Holy Spirit—help with this intimate, relational connection with God. It reminds Asian Americans that one Parent will never leave them, and they are forever a member of the Family.

Intensity. Intensity in worship is appreciated across the board by people of color and postmoderns. In our postmodern setting, worship is becoming less and less merely a song sung but an experience, a place to experience viscerally the presence of God. Thus worship songs cannot be lightly sung as if you were sitting around a campfire, or even from the head as in a more liturgical church.

For Asian Americans, worship needs to engage the heart. For most Asian Americans, worship doesn't feel like it has occurred without a sense of intensity during worship. Being authentic in worship brings an experiential and emotional intensity to worship.

To reach this level of intimacy or intensity, a great deal of trust is placed on the worship leader and the community with whom they worship. If they cannot trust either, then most Asian Americans will be unlikely to either engage *intimately* or *intensely* and thus, *freely*—three unique qualities of Asian American worship.

Preach narratively because it connects with a relational culture. It's often said that young folk are biblically illiterate. I won't argue with that but it seems less true when working with Asian Americans. They are generally more churched and "Sunday schooled" than their non-Asian counterparts, especially Korean Americans. They know John 3:16 and can tell you where to find the Psalms and 2 Timothy.

What they often lack is seeing the connection between the Bible and life. Narrative preaching can help by bridging biblical truth and their everyday experiences. When intertwined with our personal stories, Scripture's rich narratives explode with spiritual truth.

They experience being a prostitute—selling themselves off to worldly pleasures—when they hear Gomer's story retold anew with their personal challenges a part of the story. And like Gomer when she is bought back by her husband Hosea, they don't just hear about God's grace, they begin to experience it.

Or when the prodigal son's older brother is framed as the good Asian American Number One Son, they see perhaps for the first time how they have not experienced the fullness of their Father's love for them. When the older brother gets angry at his father and spits out "Look! All these years I've been slaving for you and never disobeyed your orders," it's a "been there, done that" moment for them. When the father responds with, "My son, you are always with me, and everything I have is yours," they are led to explore what "everything" includes for them.

As you "lead the emerging leaders," these and other family issues will arise. You will serve them well by not sidestepping these issues but by helping them fully engage them.

EPILOGUE

At twenty-two, I wanted to be a world-changer. At thirty-five, I wanted to build a healthier marriage, supervise well the half dozen or so for whom I was responsible and be an organization-changer. Now at fifty, I know that my best contributions will be growing into seniorland gracefully with my wife; helping our son through college and into adulthood; mentoring young leaders in their twenties and thirties and handing them the baton of leadership.

I want this last phase of ministry to be characterized by graciousness and imparting wisdom when requested to give it. My desire to be "prophetic" has waned—as I've discovered it has often been a guise for shooting people I didn't like. Now I would rather become a hope-giver, helping people lift their eyes and horizons to see all God has for their lives.

I know I have a limited number of bullets to shoot off. I want each of them to count for eternity. Being a fifty-year-old can be the death knell in a ministry focused on young people. Fortunately, Asian Americans revere and respect their elders so instead of having a weaker voice, it's stronger. I also want to be humble enough that when I am no longer effective, I will step aside rather than putting others in the awkward position of "finding another role" for me.

If you are in your twenties, what do you want to look like when you are thirty-five? If you've already arrived at that wonderful signpost, how about fifty —what do you want in your life? All of this may sound too far out there to visualize, but do pause, because this is true: *the choices we make now matter later.* A certain house bought now will impact you for thirty years (that's known as a mortgage). Choosing a certain mate impacts almost everything else you do: vocational choice, where you live, lifestyle decisions, your spiritual life.

Your life matters and your leadership matters. Out there are some Level 5 Asian American leaders. Don't make Jesus become the "hound of heaven" and have to hunt you down. Step up willingly. We need you.

The biggest challenge for the next generation of Asian American leaders is to be one.

It will be far easier to be that nail that stays hammered down. Leadership is risky, costly, dangerous and complex. It can be nerve-wracking, faith-shaking and seductive. It can drive you crazy.

You can say no. Many potentially pretty good leaders do. They just walk away and go about their business. When they do that, however, there are three losers: themselves, the lives that could have been affected by their leadership and then their followers.

Of the three, you lose the most. Being a leader stretches us to our limits and beyond. It forces us to trust God like never before. We live out faith in once invisible dimensions of our lives. We end up leading and serving some people we used to dislike even despise. We might even end up loving them.

But others lose too. You have things to give that others need; stuff you weren't even aware was yours to offer. Be that stick-out nail.

"For I know the plans I have for you," declares the LORD, "plans to prosper you and not to harm you, plans to give you hope and a future." (Jer 29:11)

You can say yes!

APPENDIX

Demographics from Census 2000

Changes in each Asian American community from 1990 to 2000

	1990	2000	Increase	% of U.S.
South Asian:	919,000	1,894,000	106%	.7%
Indian American	815,000	1,679,000	106%	.6%
Pakistani American	81,000	154,000	90%	.05%
Bangladeshi American	12,000	41,000	242%	.02%
Sri Lankan American	11,000	20,000	82%	.007%
Southeast Asian:	2,540,000	3,647,000	44%	1.3%
Filipino American	1,407,000	1,850,000	32%	.7%
Vietnamese American	615,000	1,123,000	83%	.4%
Cambodian American	147,000	172,000	17%	.06%
Hmong American	90,000	169,000	88%	.06%
Laotian American	149,000	169,000	13%	.06%
Thai American	91,000	113,000	24%	.04%
Indonesian American	29,000	40,000	38%	.01%
Malaysian American	12,000	11,000	-8%	.004%
Hawaiian/Pacific Islander	323,000	399,000	24%	.1%
East Asian:	3,293,000	4,307,000	31%	1.5%
Chinese American	1,574,000	2,315,000	47%	.8%
Korean American	799,000	1,077,000	35%	.4%
Japanese American	848,000	797,000	-6%	.3%
Taiwanese American	72,000	118,000	64%	.04%
Other Asian	780,000	1,285,000	153%	.5%
*Multiracial Asian Pacific Americans**	NA	2,132,000	—	.8%
*All Asian Pacific Americans***	7,274,000	12,773,000	69%	4.5%

*Census 2000 was the first census allowing more than one racial category to be chosen
**Includes Hawaiian/other Pacific Islanders and multiracial Asian Americans

SOUTH ASIAN AMERICANS

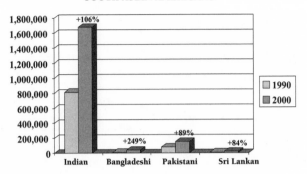

SOUTHEAST ASIAN AMERICANS

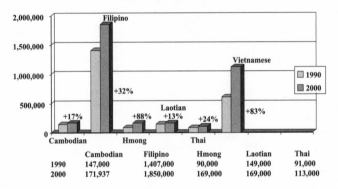

	Cambodian	Filipino	Hmong	Laotian	Thai
1990	147,000	1,407,000	90,000	149,000	91,000
2000	171,937	1,850,000	169,000	169,000	113,000

EAST ASIAN AMERICANS

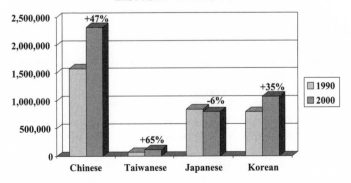

NOTES

Chapter One: Building the Spiritual Foundations of an Asian American Leader

[1]Robert Clinton, *The Making of a Leader* (Colorado Springs: NavPress, 1988), p. 44.

[2]Ibid.

Chapter Two: Understanding Our Asian DNA

[1]Lillian Hellman, *Pentimento* (Bergenfield, N.J.: New American Library, 1973), p. 1.

[2]In Sook Lee, *Korean American Ministry,* ed. San Hyun Lee and John V. Moore (Louisville, Ky.: General Assembly Council, PCUSA, 1993), p. 194.

[3]Ibid.

[4]Helen Zia, *Asian American Dreams: The Emergence of an American* People (New York: Farrar, Straus & Giroux, 2000), p. 11.

[5]Jung Young Lee, *Korean Preaching: An Interpretation* (Nashville: Abingdon, 1997), p. 37.

[6]Eunice Park, "The SATs—1500 or Bust," *AsianWeek,* October 14, 1999, p. 3.

[7]Lee, *Korean Preaching,* p. 36.

[8]Stan Inouye, "The True Samurai of God: Christ, the Cross and Culture," *The Kaki Seed,* winter 1984, p. 1.

[9]Tom Lin, *Losing Face and Finding Grace* (Downers Grove, Ill.: InterVarsity Press, 1996), p. 43.

[10]Kenneth Vyeda Fong, *Insights for Growing Asian-American Ministries* (Rosemead, Calif.: Evergrowing, 1990), p. 95.

[11]Ibid.

[12]Andrew Sung Park, *Racial Conflict and Healing* (Maryknoll, N.Y.: Orbis, 1996), p. 9.

[13]Ibid.

[14]Theodore H. White and Annalee Jacoby, *Thunder Out of China* (New York: William Sloane Associates, 1946), p. 53.

[15]Ronald Takaki, *Strangers from a Different Shore* (New York: Penguin, 1990), p. 181.

[16]Jeanette Yep, Peter Cha, Susan Cho Van Riesen, Greg Jao and Paul Tokunaga, *Following Jesus Without Dishonoring Your Parents* (Downers Grove, Ill.: InterVarsity Press, 1998).

[17]From personal communication with "David." This story has been retold with his permission.

[18]Fumitaka Matsuoka, *Out of the Silence: Emerging Themes in Asian American Churches* (Cleveland: United Church Press, 1995), p. 61.

Chapter Five: Becoming a Pretty Good Leader II
[1]"Roosevelt, Franklin Delano," in *Encarta 2000* (Redmond, Wash.: Microsoft, 1999).
[2]Truett Cathy, *It's Easier to Succeed Than to Fail* (Nashville: Oliver Nelson, 1989), p. 70.

Chapter Six: Jesus Beats the Warlords
[1]Helen Zia, *Asian American Dreams: The Emergence of an American* People (New York: Farrar, Straus & Giroux, 2000), p. 11.
[2]"Yin and Yang," in *Encarta 2000* (Redmond, Wash.: Microsoft, 1999).
[3]James C. Collins and Jerry I. Porras, *Built to Last: Successful Habits of Visionary Companies* (New York: HarperBusiness Essentials, 1994), p. 80.
[4]Takie Sugiyama Lebra, *Japanese Patterns of Behavior* (Honolulu: University of Hawaii Press, 1976), p. 38.
[5]Rebecca Manley Pippert, *Out of the Saltshaker,* rev. ed. (Downers Grove, Ill.: InterVarsity Press, 1999), p. 34.

Chapter Seven: New Biblical Paradigms for Leadership
[1]Hazel Offner, *Moses: A Man Changed by God* (Downers Grove, Ill.: InterVarsity Press, 1981, pp. 50-51.
[2]Marian Wright Edelman, *Lanterns: A Memoir to Mentors* (Boston: Beacon, 1999), pp. 117-18.

Chapter Eight: Becoming a Really Good Leader
[1]Takie Sugiyama Lebra, *Japanese Patterns of Behavior* (Honolulu: University of Hawaii Press, 1976), p. 40.
[2]Cited by Helen Lee in "Silent Exodus: Can the East Asian Church in America Reverse the Flight of Its Next Generation?" *Christianity Today,* August 12, 1996, p. 52.

Chapter Nine: Becoming a Great Leader
[1]Jim Collins, "Level 5 Leadership: The Triumph of Humility and Fierce Resolve," *Harvard Business Review,* January 2001, p. 67.
[2]Jim Collins, *Good to Great* (New York: HarperBusiness, 2001), p. 20.
[3]Collins, "Level 5 Leadership," p. 68.
[4]Collins, *Good to Great,* p. 18.
[5]Ibid., p. 28.
[6]Ibid.
[7]Ibid., p. 37, emphasis in original.

Chapter Eleven: Big Numbers That Breathe and Bleed
[1]The U.S. Census Bureau uses the following designations: *Asian*—A person having origins in any of the original peoples of the Far East, Southeast Asia or the Indian subcontinent,

including, for example, Cambodia, China, India, Japan, Korea, Malaysia, Pakistan, the Philippine Islands, Thailand and Vietnam. It includes "Asian Indian," "Chinese," "Filipino," "Korean," "Japanese," "Vietnamese" and "Other Asian." *Native Hawaiian and Other Pacific Islander*—A person having origins in any of the original peoples of Hawaii, Guam, Samoa or other Pacific Islands. It includes people who indicate their race as "Native Hawaiian," "Guamanian or Chamooro," "Samoan" and "Other Pacific Islander."

[2]Percentages are rounded to the nearest point; some lists may thus total more (or less) than 100 percent.

[3]Ken Fong, *Pursuing the Pearl* (Valley Forge, Penn.: Judson, 1999), p. 47.

[4]Eugene Peterson, *Run with the Horses* (Downers Grove, Ill.: InterVarsity Press, 1983), p. 162.

[5]Herman Melville, *The Confidence-Man* (New York: Signet Classics, 1964), p. 119.

Chapter Twelve: Different, Sometimes Way Different

[1]Harry Kitano and Roger Daniels, *Asian Americans: Emerging Minorities* (Englewood Cliffs, N.J.: Prentice-Hall, 1988), p. 191.

Chapter Thirteen: Telling the Truth About Asian American Secrets

[1]Ken Fong, *Pursuing the Pearl* (Valley Forge, Penn.: Judson, 1999), p. 25.

[2]Cited in Helen Lee, "Silent Exodus," *Christianity Today,* August 12, 1996, p. 52.

[3]Ibid., p. 50.

[4]Ibid., p. 51.

[5]Ibid.

[6]Ibid.

[7]Ibid., p. 52.

[8]David Gibbons, interviewed by Helen Lee, *re:generation quarterly* 5, no. 3 (1999): n.p.

[9]Lee, "Silent Exodus," p. 53.

[10]Fong, *Pursuing the Pearl*, p. 105.

[11]Jung Ha Kim, "The Labor of Compassion: Voices of Churched Korean American Women," in *New Spiritual Homes: Religion and Asian Americans,* ed. David K. Yoo (Honolulu: University of Hawaii Press, 1999), p. 207.